and
Detectives

Some Other Books
by Ken Worpole

Reading by Numbers

Towns for People

**Libraries in a World
of Cultural Change**
(with Liz Greenhalgh & Charles Landry)

Staying Close to the River

**Here Comes the Sun:
Architecture & Public Space in
Twentieth-Century European Culture**

**Last Landscapes:
the Architecture of the Cemetery
in the West**

350 Miles
(with photographer Jason Orton)

Dockers
and
Detectives

Ken Worpole

Five Leaves Publications
info@fiveleaves.co.uk
www.fiveleaves.co.uk

Dockers and Detectives

2nd edition
Ken Worpole

Published in 2008 by Five Leaves Publications, PO Box 8786,
Nottingham NG1 9AW
info@fiveleaves.co.uk
www.fiveleaves.co.uk

ISBN: 978 1 905512 37 9

Five Leaves acknowledges financial support
from Arts Council England

Cover illustration:
A view of shipping and lighterage in the Royal Albert Dock, 1958.
Photographed by Endicott for the PLA.
Reproduced courtesy of the Museum of London.

The first edition of Dockers and Detectives
was published by Verso in 1983

Five Leaves is a member of Inpress
(www.inpressbooks.co.uk),
representing independent publishers

Design and typesetting by Four Sheets Design and Print
Printed in Great Britain

Contents

Acknowledgements

I would like to thank a number of people without whose help this book would not have been published: Ross Bradshaw at Five Leaves Press, for the efficient enthusiasm with which the whole process has been conducted; Ken Clay, Andy Croft, Alan Dent, Christopher Hilliard, Rebecca O'Rourke, Jenny Hartley and Tony Wailey, who all answered questions or provided helpful comments or additional references; Giles O'Bryen of Verso for expediting rights issues, and Neil Belton, the original editor, who first encouraged the book into being. During the period of revising the text, I was fortunate in receiving a grant from the Society of Authors, to whom gratitude is expressed. Final thanks are due to Larraine Worpole as always: for support, forbearance, love and comradeship in this and everything else.

Dig Where You Stand
A new introduction to *Dockers and Detectives*

Dockers and Detectives was first written before the psycho-geographers were abroad, and when historical and literary endeavour took everyday life as meaningful imaginative territory.[1] I was then closely involved in a number of writing and local history projects in Hackney. One of the rallying cries of the History Workshop movement at that time had been, "Dig Where You Stand", an exhortation to renew history through local research and exegesis. Such an approach required finding out what had gone before, and thus an interest in writers of Hackney and London's East End from earlier periods in the twentieth-century began to engage me. What was happening in Hackney was part of a much wider movement to create, or re-create, a different kind of radical politics based on history and identity, place and memory.

The background reading which occasioned these essays was first done in the 1970s and early 1980s, and they are re-published more or less unchanged except for some minor re-writing to make the text clearer, or to take into account new information which has emerged since. Though all of the chapters deal with the role that the reading and writing of fiction played in people's sense of themselves and their history in the decades preceding and following the Second World War (which for my post-war generation was an emotional and intellectual anchoring), some deal with fictional representations of politics and locality, while others look at the political and class issues inherent in emerging forms of genre fiction characteristic of the time.

A Question of Class, A Question of Place
The principal literary and cultural locales highlighted in two of the essays, London's East End and Liverpool's

7

docklands, had in the 20th century been both celebrated and denigrated — the latter, invariably from outside. Yet the imaginative hold these places exercised upon their inhabitants at particular moments in history were deep and pervasive, and in both cases I knew them well, having lived and worked in both. Few regions or urban settlements have possessed quite the same sense of identity and intensity in the first half of the twentieth-century, which partly explains why they were so productive and creative in the writing they produced. Both were, significantly, port cities, with much coming and going, but also with emphatic and deeply held religious and political affiliations.

In the wider literary world, the concern with what is often regarded as place-based writing, whether fictional, historical or topographical, is usually grouped under the term "regionalism", and remains a minor area of literary interest or concern. This is perhaps why some of the writers resurrected in *Dockers and Detectives* were forgotten so quickly. Regionalism often functions as a way of avoiding the difficult issue of writing about class and, more recently, ethnicity and race. In terms of the books and writers discussed, the "hidden injuries of class" were dominant themes of the writing, and were often internalised as a heightened form of vulnerability and individual self-doubt, leading to vistas of escape and re-settlement. One of the forms of escape was reading, another was writing, and a third was an attachment to militant left-wing politics.

It is hard for many people today to understand, let alone sympathise with, a certain kind of revolutionary millenarianism that haunted the further reaches of left-wing politics for much of the 20th century, and which was an underlying motif in much of the writing represented here.[2] It was an established part of socialist and communist belief that the industrial working-class had been given the historical role of transforming society from a capitalist one to one built on the principles of socialism, and ultimately communism. It is also worth remembering that the British

Communist Party itself — certainly in the 1930s when many of the writers discussed here were at their peak — was overwhelmingly working-class in membership.[3] Well into the 1970s it remained the case that not only within the Communist Party, but also in parts of the Labour Party, there was an inherited assumption that the working-class enjoyed a privileged — later termed "redemptive" — role in the long march of history.

The rise of the History Workshop movement was part of that redemptive teleology, and involved recovering lost evidence of working-class culture and self-organisation of those hidden from history, the recording of which would contribute to a fuller sense of the historic role still to be played by the working-class at the moment of their final rendezvous with history. The publication in 1968 of E.P. Thompson's *The Making of the English 'Working Class'* only fuelled this sense of a destiny in the making, as Thompson seemed to discern within a myriad of events, upheavals, demonstrations and insurrections from the 1790s onwards, a class "present at its own making", self-organised, self-conscious, and with its own historical destiny to fulfil. For a while the rapid spread of the people's history movement, with shock troops firmly entrenched at Ruskin College, Oxford, seemed to mark a new beginning. In retrospect, it has been argued, it was only the beginning of the end.

In December 2006, at a gathering to commemorate the 10th anniversary of the death of the charismatic social historian and guiding figure of the History Workshop movement, Raphael Samuel, a younger historian, James Vernon, gave a sober critique of the people's history movement, arguing that,

> ...the History Workshop version of people's history was a product of the crisis of social democracy. Rather than just enabling people to recover their history, it endeavoured to tell the subaltern to speak at the precise moment when their class destiny was historically faltering.[4]

For Vernon the movement was linked to the fortunes of the social democratic state, and came only in time to remind people of the historic achievements of British working-class movements and politics, just as social democracy breathed its last gasp, and mainstream political parties across Europe attached themselves to the same global market consensus and "the end of ideology". Vernon's assessment seems mostly right to me, and also helps explain why some of the vocabulary of *Dockers and Detectives* now seems to come not only from another time, but another political planet.

The Un-making of the English Working-class?

Both Jonathan Rose and Christopher Hilliard, in their recent accounts of British working-class intellectual life and reading, assume that history has now ended.[5] Furthermore, the very material landscapes of those lives and cultures are themselves being swept away without any regard for the heritage they embodied, as is so clearly described in a haunting paragraph by the historian Robert Colls, from his book, *Identity of England*:

> When the staple northern industries began to splutter from the 1970s, very deep meanings choked with them. Buildings that for years had given habitude to landscape were brought down without a second glance. Elegant mill chimneys, dramatic colliery headgear, sun-bright ship-yard cranes, all hit the ground in clouds of masonry, and with them fell a whole visual culture. Where ships' hulls had once swerved across the skyline, there was now only sky. Lodges and institutes, formerly places of association and learning, became derelict. The bands ceased to march. Banners were furled. Methodist chapels, emotional heart-lands of the Industrial Revolution, became carpet stores. Pine pews were ripped out and sold as antiques. A land-scape was humiliated, piecemeal.[6]

While the buildings, gardens and artefacts of the pre-industrial world and land-owning classes are studiously preserved, there remains a cavalier attitude to the indus-trial heritage, and to the material cultures of working people and the singular worlds they created and inhabited. Historians have too turned their gaze away from the history of class and politics, so that today we seem to know more about 18th century markets in glassware and other luxury goods than we do about late 19th and early 20th century struggles for popular democracy.

Yet every so often class raises its head anew, angrily and bitterly around issues of place, identity and memory. When Glasgow was declared European City of Culture in 1990, a group of trades unionists, writers and artists calling themselves "Workers City" issued a ferocious attack on those definitions of culture which excluded a full recognition of Glasgow's troubled and highly radicalised working-class life and history. The same happened again when Liverpool was declared European City of Culture for 2008: poets, playwrights, artists, novelists and local political activists insisted that the rich history of Liverpool's maritime and industrial culture should be fully reflected in the celebrations. Likewise a bitter controversy over the post-war cultural history of one of London's most distinctive working-class districts has recently been provoked by the publication of a provocative sociological study, *The New East End*.[7] Folklore has become the last redoubt of working-class identity in many but not all British cities, taking symbolic shape in the streetscapes and landscapes of remembered places.

From early on class was interwoven with place, with localism, with street life and even with landscape. Clerkenwell's printers and instrument-makers lived in a world as different as it is possible to be from that of Welsh miners, Tyneside ship-builders, or Lancashire's cotton workers. Even as late as the 1950s, London's dockers and lightermen inhabited rituals and customs, quite unlike those of Cornwall's tin-miners, Bolton's mill girls, Irish construction workers or London's East End Jewish cabinet-makers and tailors. Yet the institutions and moral economies they each and separately created locally, and the principles upon which these were based, led to national and international movements. The British working-class became one of the most dynamic social forces of the industrial world, admired and emulated across the globe, pioneering the creation of trade unions, the international Co-operative movement along with a politics based on traditions of self-education, mutual aid and internationalism. It also produced a literature and historical narrative of its own making and meaning.

This history has now been relegated to the margins of cultural memory. Today the institutions of the wider labour movement, and the values which created and sustained, them have been declared redundant — outmoded forms of mutual aid in a world of economic models based solely on private actors and their interests (even as, paradoxically, politicians scramble round in the bargain basement of "communitarian" theory for ways of evoking and recreating desperately needed new forms of social responsibility and moral solidarity).

Furthermore the geography of class has changed dramatically. As Lynsey Hanley has written in her graphic account of post-war housing policy, the large-scale redevelopment of many towns and cities not only removed working-class communities from their historic inner-city territory, but in creating vast peripheral housing estates, ended up stigmatising them too, as marginal or surplus peoples.[8] The Becontree Estate was built to house (or exile) 120,000 East Londoners; Norris Green took 50,000 inner-city residents of Liverpool and located them on the edge of the city, cut off from their historic economic and social networks. So while class still exerts a powerful influence on many people's attitudes, aspirations and career choices, its relationship to radical politics and affiliations of place is now attenuated.

Distant Voices, Real Lives

In the 1970s, many people were struck by parallels between that decade and that of the 1930s, culturally and politically. The wish to create a more representative literary culture was common to both. In 1971, Angus Wilson and Malcolm Bradbury founded the School of Creative Writing at the University of East Anglia. This became the subject of much derision from established literary quarters. Writing, it was claimed, was something that could not be taught. These sentiments remain close to the surface of influential elements of literary life, yet to those of us teaching English in schools at this time, it was a denial of basic common sense — in fact it was what we were paid for and expected to do. Creative writing classes have flourished ever since, particularly so in America. When in early 2007 *Granta* magazine announced its Best of Young American Novelists list, chosen by a heavyweight panel of British and American critics chaired by Ian Jack, the panel noted that most selected had attended creative writing courses or writing school.[9]

In the very same year as the setting up of the East Anglian academic experiment in 1971, a communist activist, Ben Ainley, started an English class at New Cross Ward Labour Club, in Manchester, intended not only to encourage the reading and discussion of literature, but the writing of it as well. Out of these gatherings emerged occasional duplicated magazines of poetry and fiction, and thus *Voices*, a magazine of working-class writing, was born. This ran for more than a decade, eventually becoming a national magazine.[10] *Voices*, and the title was significant, published the work of over 250 first-time writers, many from the North West of England. These included coal-miners, peace activists, union officials, students, railway workers, park-keepers, teachers and lorry-drivers, former International Brigaders, shipyard workers and many labour movement activists. The early work of John Cooper Clarke (one of *Voices'* founding members), Jimmy McGovern and Tony Marchant first appeared in its pages.

The work of these three is interesting not simply because they all achieved national recognition — the first as poet and musician, the other two as highly acclaimed television dramatists — but because all three displayed an acute attentiveness to the dramatic qualities of working-class speech. In this there was a continuation of a tradition started by that earlier generation of writers — Alexander Baron, Simon Blumenfeld, James Hanley, Emanuel Litvinoff and Frank Tilsley — whose work is examined later in these pages. They wrote for the theatre, radio and television (and a number of whom also started out in writers' circles).[11] Indeed, Frank Tilsley is credited with being the writer of the first "soap opera" for television, *The Makepeace Story*, a saga about a Lancashire cotton family serialized in 1955, and gaining an audience of eight million viewers, a precursor to "Coronation Street", on which Jimmy McGovern learned his script-writing trade.

In their later years, both Hanley and Baron became successful broadcast dramatists. Christopher Hilliard's book on the "democratization of writing in Britain", draws attention to the close relationship between writers' circles and amateur dramatic groups in regional Britain, noting that in 1949, Liverpool alone had more than 300 local drama groups.[12] If there is any one quality which characterises much of the writing from and about working-class life — whether in the form of poems, short stories, diaries, letters, novels — it was, and remains, the centrality of the human voice. That voice often spoke in a local or regional dialect.

The principal carrier of this tradition since has been James Kelman, the Scottish novelist whose series of short story collections and novels has often involved a dialect-speaking protagonist raging against the poverty and injustices of working-class life.[13] Kelman's work tends to be handled cautiously, even at arm's length, by metropolitan reviewers, though they recognise a distinctive talent when they see it: Kelman won the Booker Prize in 1994 with his novel, *How Late It Was, How Late*. Kelman's literary style is at times uncompromising, taking the form of a continuous dialect monologue in many stories, but it summons up a way of life and an attitude to life (not unlike the work of Thomas Bernhard) that is insistent and unforgiving.[14] Nor should one forget the work of Harold

Pinter, whose early short plays drew their dramatic atmosphere from the puzzled human speech and non-sequiturs of ill-met exchanges in working-class cafés and boarding houses dotted around the streets of London's East End.

Yet while class never goes away in British life, the representation of working-class life tends today towards either nostalgia or contempt (though some would say it was ever thus). On television, apart from the work of McGovern, Marchant, and one or two others, portrayals of working-class life have retreated, as they so often have in the past, to fear and loathing, or of comic capers. Early in his career Bill Naughton wrote that, "almost every portrayal of working-class life and people that I'd read was a travesty. No wonder the different classes had such absurd notions of how one another lived." He could have been writing today. Working class life and experience are as inadequately represented today politically and culturally as in the days of Naughton, a situation which is once again becoming the subject of debate.[15] Nor did anyone anticipate the rise of "misery lit" as a best-selling genre: harrowing stories of brutalised childhoods, often eloquently and passionately narrated, but invariably focusing on the condition of victimhood, rarely making any connection to wider social conditions, as if in the end the world was really a feral war of all against all.

Voices not only published new writing, but carried discussions about mainstream writers admired by readers as sound literary models, and what styles and forms best suited the aspiring writer. This abiding interest in what people read and write remains a mainstream element in intellectual and social history. Since *Dockers and Detectives* was first published, there has been a sequence of fascinating (even if sometimes overly academic) books on the subject, including Valentine Cunningham's *British Writers of the Thirties* (1988), Alan Munton's *English Fiction of the Second World War* (1989), Mark Rawlinson's *British Writing of the Second World War* (2000), Andy Croft's *Red*

Letters: British Fiction in the 1930s (1990), John Carey's *The Intellectuals and the Masses* (1992), Adam Piette's *Imagination at War* (1995), John Lucas's *Radical Twenties* (1997), Jenny Hartley's *Millions Like Us: British Women's Fiction of the Second World War* (1997), Valerie A. Reeves and Valerie Showan's *Dan Billany: Hull's Lost Hero* (1999), Dorothy Sheridan's *Wartime Women* (2000), Jonathan Rose's *The Intellectual Life of the British Working Classes* (2001), John Fordham's *James Hanley: Modernism and the Working Class* (2002), Sukhdev Sandhu's, *London Calling: How Black and Asian Writers Imagined a City*, (2003), and Christopher Hilliard's *To Exercise Our Talents: the Democratisation of Writing in Britain* (2006).

Other writers such as Robert Hewison, H.Gustav Klaus, Rebecca O'Rourke, Paul Lester, Iain Sinclair and Patrick Wright have all made thoughtful contributions to our knowledge of these themes. The very lexicon at use in such titles and sub-titles — British, English, Writing, Fiction, Literature, Masses, Working Classes — is a reminder of how complex and problematic these terms are, and the particular cultural and historical tensions they suggest when yoked together. Neither too should we forget that there was a time when the notion of "the common reader" lay at the heart of literary criticism and debate: no longer.

Critical Responses

A number of the studies mentioned above explicitly referred to the issues raised in *Dockers and Detectives*, and helped shed further light on the work of Alexander Baron, Dan Billany, Simon Blumenfeld, George Garrett, James Hanley, Emanuel Litvinoff, and Jim Phelan. The books about Dan Billany and James Hanley were particularly welcome. Of course nobody can actually "discover" the work of writers once published and acclaimed; they can only be "re-remembered" (to adapt one of Iain Sinclair's apt tropes). Even so, *Dockers and Detectives* did instigate some new ways of thinking about who and what gets

16

published at particular moments of great social upheaval, as well as encouraging the re-valuation (a typically Leavisite notion) of some remarkably original writers whose work had passed out of critical memory. Certainly the book contributed to a revival of interest in Baron, Billany, Blumenfeld, Goldman, Hanley and Litvinoff, and new editions of books by them have since been published.[16]

Yet even with these studies, the selective tradition still exists, especially within the academy. Valentine Cunningham's canonical and ostensibly definitive account of British writers in the 1930s, nevertheless fails to mention the work of Mark Benney, James Curtis, Gerald Kersh, Frank Tilsley (a prolific, uneven, but occasionally great writer about working-class life and politics), or Robert Westerby. Yet these writers are now regarded as cult novelists of the period, whose work is still resonant today. Adam Piette's *Imagination at War*, presented as a comprehensive account of British fiction and poetry of the Second World War, nevertheless fails to refer to the work of Alexander Baron, rightly described by John Williams as "the greatest British novelist of the last war and among the finest, most underrated, of the post war period."[17] Billany is only briefly referred to, though his prison diaries and notebooks exemplify to perfection what Piette claimed to be his principal concern: "...the mind talking to itself, in the form of essay, poem, novel, diary, letter."[18]

Billany's work touched me more than any other, as I read his posthumously published novels in the gloom of the old British Library. Then one day, shortly after the publication of *Dockers and Detectives*, I was sent a parcel out of the blue containing the original notebooks for *The Trap*. These hand-written exercise books had been compiled in an Italian prisoner-of-war camp in 1943, and passed on to an Italian farmer for safe-keeping when Billany had escaped, only to die — from exposure in the Appennines it is thought — shortly after. At the end of the war, the farmer had sent the notebooks to Billany's family address, where they arrived on 21st March 1946. In fact the texts for two novels were contained in the notebooks, and both were eventually published as *The Cage* and *The Trap*, in 1949 and 1950 respectively. I had been sent them by Billany's sister, Mrs Joan Brake, after I had learnt of her existence and sent her a copy of *Dockers and Detectives*. Soon after my wife and I were invited to visit her home in Somerset, partly to help annotate all of Billany's poems, letters and unpublished writings, which were eventually given to the Imperial War Museum. We became good friends.

It was fascinating, at the time of publication of *Dockers and Detectives*, to discover which of the book's principal themes or arguments engaged reviewers, in what was an exploratory series of essays peering into forgotten corners of the British literary past. In *New Society*, Raymond Williams welcomed the book keenly, while suggesting that certain ideas latent in it were still in need of much further work and clarification.[19] The first of these questions was one of terminology and definition: what is it precisely that makes popular literature popular? Is the very concept of popular literature (now, interestingly, much less used in literary circles) a matter of sales figures, status of readership, or of genre? This was a crucial question, still only partially answered.

My intuitive sense of what was meant by "popular literature" had its origins in the fables, stories, mythologies and epics of early print culture — which had later developed into mainstream fictional forms. As an English teacher I had spent much of my reading time absorbed in children's literature and that influence was always just beneath the surface. When I used the term "popular literature" in *Dockers and Detectives* I implied that it came from within the historic tradition of story-telling concerned with ordinary people and their lives, often in the form of a heightened or self-mythologising realism. The books examined had mostly been written by those who had directly experienced the events described, not at one remove. There was usually only one coat of literary paint

18

covering the surface of life as felt and lived. These included novels written by seamen, by those who had directly experienced war, by the inhabitants of particular communities about their lives and neighbourhoods: all adhered to this definition, and indeed drew much of their energy and style from these popular narrative traditions.

Another issue raised by Williams referred to this complicated category of "the regional". Williams rejected the concept of the region (not surprisingly, since the term had so often been used to dismiss whole nations such as his own, Wales, as simply a regional construct). He wrote that:

> For these writers, in different ways, belonged to more local worlds, and it has been my own experience that it is only in such localities — what the centralised mind calls regions — that these writers are, if at all, remembered and valued. This in turn feeds the prejudices of the literary establishment: to be working-class and regional is a double default.[20]

As was observed earlier, regionalism was also used as a way of avoiding direct engagement with issues of class. In the last decades of the twentieth-century the term "local" became yet another synonym for "working-class", once again, and misleadingly, conflating two different categories of experience entirely.

Yet regionalism, in my view, continues to embody real energies and mature structures of feeling, though it was, and is, much more convincingly used as a credible and persuasive literary mode in North America, where the geographical scale of regionalism is much greater. Many of the radical cultural and political energies of the left in America in the 1930s were absorbed into the creation of regional forms of expression: folklore, music, photography, poetry, documentary and fictional writing, notably through the efforts of various public agencies of the New Deal, such as the Civil Works Administration, the Public Works of Art Project, the Federal Art Project, the Federal

Writers' Project and even the Farm Security Administration.[21] The Federal Writers' Project alone employed at its height over 6,700 writers, clerks, typists and others, including Nelson Algren, Conrad Aiken, Saul Bellow, John Cheever, Studs Terkel and helped give an impetus to black writers such as Richard Wright and Ralph Ellison.

No such schemes occurred in Britain, though it is true that, as Christopher Hilliard has argued, many local writers' circles took a particular interest in "safeguarding a locale's literary tradition".[22] He also makes the interesting point, though fails to elaborate upon it, that regionalism in Britain was undermined by "the decline of Nonconformity after 1900".[23] We can only assume he refers to the close relationship between Nonconformist religion and municipal civic politics, which began to ebb away as national party politics took over the local stage. Efforts to create a regionalism of culture and identity in Britain similar to that in the USA were, paradoxically, largely in the hands of communists and anarchists, who for different reasons, cultivated a culture based on the experiences of those who lived closest to the ground.

There was one notable exception to the lack of British equivalents to the Federal Writers' Project, and that was Mass Observation. Founded in Britain in 1937 by anthropologist Tom Harrisson, poet Charles Madge and film-maker Humphrey Jennings, the organisation recruited some 500 untrained volunteers to keep diaries and report on everyday life, often around designated themes. Although the project ended in the 1950s it was revived in 1981 and is now administered from the University of Sussex, where the archives are housed (and increasingly sifted for the richness of the material by historians and literary anthologists). In recent years books based on the use of M-O archive material, such as *Nella Last's War, Millions Like Us* and *Wartime Women* have proved of enormous public interest and historical importance. More recent collections of M-O diaries, edited by Simon Garfield, have further opened up our view of what life was like in the 1930s and 1940s, and David Kynaston's much acclaimed history of the period, *Austerity Britain 1945-51*, could not have been written without extensive drawing on M-O materials.[24] Though the work of Mass Observation has remained the subject of some methodological scepticism — about the motives and veracity of those contributing — this scepticism could be applied to all forms of documentation and testimony. In the end, all intellectual enquiry and testimony is *parti pris*.

What Remains?

The essays which follow dealt with different aspects of popular reading and writing. The first two looked critically at distinctive new genres of popular fiction which came to prominence from the 1930s onwards, and particularly after the Second World War: the "tough-guy novel" imported from America, and the popular literature devoted to the human experience of the Second World War. The subsequent two looked at specific schools of "regional" writing: in the work of a small group of Liverpool-Irish seamen, and in the Jewish writers of London's East End.

Thus the sense of "popular" being used, and questioned by Williams, involved issues of genre (the detective novel as an example of popular fiction), large readership figures (the war books sold widely and for a long time), modern re-workings of the Homeric epic (the sailor's story as an enduring type of popular mythology), and the daily life of the working-class neighbourhood or ghetto (the Jewish East End as an exemplary life of a people). These all involve inflections of the "popular", but in ways which I think it will always be impossible to completely untangle, other than the fact that nearly all of the books discussed were written by people who did not come from traditional literary or intellectual elites. As the French cultural commentator Pierre Bourdieu once noted, the literary forms developed by auto-didacts, or the conventionally unschooled, often cross boundaries, and make them somewhat resistant to traditional critical responses.

Many of the issues raised are still in play. Thus there is still a continuing debate about the influence of American writing (and popular culture) on British cultural life, a subject I had first become interested in when teaching English, and like many teachers found that young people responded to the apparently artless style of Hemingway in the famous "Nick Adams" stories. Later on, chance conversations with a number of elderly working-class trades unionists made me realise just how refreshing they had found American fiction — often mentioning the work of Theodore Dreiser, Upton Sinclair, Ernest Hemingway or Raymond Chandler for example — compared with English fiction of the same period. It was not just about subject matter, but also about the directness of the literary style. This was part of a wider mood of admiration for all things American — democracy, culture, political institutions, landscape — which affected many British people from the moment of that country's first inception, as Jonathan Rose has demonstrated.[25]

Even so, there has still been a tendency to ignore the positive aspects of this cultural transmigration, regarding the American influence on British culture in the post-war period as essentially corrupt. This remains the view of Ross McKibbin, one of the most assiduous historians of 20th Century working-class life and culture, following many of the same arguments as Ronald Blythe and Richard Hoggart had done in earlier times, with their throwaway remarks about the "school of sex and guns".[26]

Yet with the benefit of hindsight, we can see that there was an American tradition of writing about both urban and rural life — notwithstanding an overt masculinity — that was sensitive to everyday emotional experience. This empathy with the lives of ordinary people has continued to underscore American literature even to this day, in the work of writers such as Raymond Carver, Richard Ford, Richard Yates and the school of writing subsequently styled "dirty realism". There is no contemporary equivalent in Britain — in fiction at least — though elements of it are strongly represented in television drama. While that American school of writing is slowly being superseded — or so it might appear from the *Granta* list of promising young American novelists mentioned earlier — it is still refreshing to hear a writer like Richard Ford speak so eloquently even today on matters of class and empathy:

> My view, and it's a kind of hopeful, progressive, humanist's view, is that anybody embedded in his or her life — a railroad worker, a ditch digger, whatever the hell — has more to offer us than we think they do. People have rich interior lives. People have possibilities that we don't, on the basis of convention, ever accord to them. Who are we to say someone who works on the railroad isn't going to have a rich interior life? That seems to me to be cynical about human beings.[27]

Another concern was the degree to which working-class cultural movements in the twentieth-century clung to traditional forms, and eschewed any attachment to modernism. "When workers write poetry," the French historian Michelet once wrote, "they put on gloves." In the chapter on Garrett, Hanley and Phelan, I argued that these three writers had been deeply influenced by expressionist experiments in drama, fiction and even the cinema, and that their writing styles demonstrated this. Since then John Fordham has written definitively about Hanley's deep immersion in modernist ideas and writings, while the intellectual milieux in which Garrett and Phelan found themselves at times (including Phelan reading Döblin in prison) have since been understood as steeped in a wide, cosmopolitan, literary culture, often through the independent left-wing and literary bookshops they attached themselves to, as well as the public libraries where some congregated.[28]

However, Jonathan Rose insists that British working-class writers and intellectuals disdained modernist forms and devices. He writes, for example, that "working-class cultural conservatism also manifested itself in total resistance to modern music, which never enjoyed a place in the brass band repertory."[29] While that may be true of the 1930s — though I remain sceptical — in post-war Britain the brass band movement went out of its way to explore new music. In his oral history of this movement, *Labour & Love*, Arthur R. Taylor interviewed a number of factory band arrangers and conductors, all of whom spoke with enthusiasm about having commissioned new works by Thea Musgrave, Harrison Birtwhistle, and Hans Werner Henze — all eminent and supposedly "difficult" modern composers.[30]

Rose's position has also been addressed by Christopher Hilliard, in an essay which details the way in which a number of working-class writers of the 1930s came to admire some of the more experimental European writing published by John Lehmann in *New Writing*, admitting however that where other working-class auto-didacts may have found the work of Eliot, Joyce and Woolf difficult and esoteric, in this they were no different from the middle-brow reading public, which disliked such writers equally.[31]

Then there is also the question of where working-class women, as readers and writers, fitted into the wider picture of picture of 1930's literary and political culture. The absence of any detailed discussion of women's writing was explicitly acknowledged in the book, being beyond the scope of these particular essays. Yet of course it remains an issue of outstanding interest and cultural importance, though one that is now being increasingly addressed in some detail. Even at the time of writing I knew that Rebecca O'Rourke was already working on the subject, and later published a crucial essay called, "Were there no women?"[32]

O'Rourke's essay pointed, as one reason amongst others, to the lack of patronage which working-class women might expect in comparison to men. As Andy Croft recorded elsewhere of the working-class male writers,

"Brierley was helped by Hampson, Walter Greenwood was helped by Ethel Mannin; Julius Lipton by Cecil Day Lewis; Harry Heslop by Harold Shaylor; Jack Hilton, Jack Common and 'Roger Dataller' by Middleton Murray; George Garrett and B.L. Coombes by John Lehmann, and so on."[33] Patronage for the men also came from organisations such as Ruskin College or the National Union of Miners. For many years there was even an annual literary prize just for fiction or essays written by miners — the Arthur Markham Prize — astonishing though that might seem today. These personal, financial and institutional forms of support were lacking for women, according to O'Rourke:

> There were no women in the NUM, a union which took a strong encouraging stand to develop pride and confidence in working-class writing; there were no women students at Ruskin; no women in the reading room of the Whitechapel Library; no women out of work with the idleness in direct proportion to their rage against the system.[34]

There were some attempts to remedy this situation. Andy Croft found evidence that, "After the success of *Seven Shifts* (Jack Common's edited collection of essays on working-class trades, all by men, published in 1938) Common and Jack Hilton began editing a sequel about women's work", though this along with a number of other projects failed to reach completion.[35] (Many years later, in the early 1970s, "The People's Autobiography of Hackney" group, in which I was closely involved, published two volumes of *Working Lives,* greatly influenced by Common's pioneering collection, though this time women's work was represented in equal proportion.[36])

Not only were women invisible in work, they were also invisible at home, where their efforts to maintain a home, to bear children and provide food, comfort and support, was hardly considered as meaningful activity, let alone of political consequence. So whilst the degradation of unemployment is a frequent theme of male writing, it was regarded as beyond the experience of women as O'Rourke observes:

> Unemployment even now appears as something which doesn't happen to women. Because women don't work, or if they do, don't do proper jobs, or are only doing them until they have kids, they cannot ever lose, or be denied them.[37]

Her essay also highlighted the crucial issues of literary form and gender — noting that women's writing historically had often been confined, under various pressures, to letters and diaries — and was vindicated as various publications emerged from the vaults of the Mass-Observation archives, most notably in the publication *of Nella Last's Diary 1939-45* in 1981, mentioned earlier. There were also publications from the Co-operative Women's Guild, encouraging and commissioning accounts from women of all classes about their daily lives.

Since then Jenny Hartley's study, *Millions Like Us*, has explored the subject even more fully, paying attention to the forms, genres, and framing devices of women's writing during the Second World War.[38] Of particular concern to Hartley has been the wish to re-instate the importance of the personal letter as a vital medium of record and personal expression, often a form favoured by women, especially under the conditions of war and separation.[39] Even before the war a Co-operative Correspondence Club had been established in 1935 to establish contact between women "trapped" at home, though this was primarily aimed at professional women who had been forced to give up their jobs on marriage or as a result of having children.[40] It is worth recording that Flora Thompson, whose trilogy *Lark Rise to Candleford*, achieved immediate literary success as a finely wrought account of rural life and poverty, had started work as an assistant post-mistress, a remarkable woman for whom the writing and receiving of letters was in her lifeblood from the beginning to the end of her life.

Hartley's essay, "Letters are everything these days", enumerates just how intense was the act of letter-writing during the conditions of war. From March 1944 to March 1945, 374 million letters were despatched overseas from Britain, the majority of them written by women.[41] It was women, Hartley suggests, "who seem to see the point of letters, to have grasped their power and seized their possibilities with particular zest." Much of this power was directed towards recreating the conditions and memories of home for men and women fighting overseas, desperately trying to keep up morale at both ends of the epistolary journey, in what Hartley calls "the real people's novels of the war, optimistic and positive, long-running hope operas."

In the end, though, all history is contemporary history, a narrative in which all the jigsaw pieces of the past — events, lives, narratives, beliefs — are reconfigured and interpreted by each generation anew, in the attempt to provide a coherent foundation for an understanding as to how present circumstances came to be. As was observed at the outset, historians and writers in the 1970s became immensely interested in re-visiting the politics and aesthetics of the 1930s. In recent times politicians of all parties have been fighting over the political and cultural legacy of the 1960s, arguing as to whether it was the beginning of a new era of enlightened social attitudes and freedom of expression, or the moment when the rot set in, and the institutions of traditional life and culture were undermined from without and within.

Issues of place and identity are again foremost amongst the political and cultural issues of the day. The 1997 Labour Government began the long process of devolution of power to the nations of the Union, with Scottish and Welsh parliaments and assemblies created, leaving an unresolved problem as to the residual identity of England itself. Both the Scottish and Welsh literatures of place now seem stronger and more continuous than the English tradition of writing about place and cultural identity — particularly where matters of class are concerned. At the heart of the English dilemma is what is increasingly perceived as the writing out of history of the English working-class, a class on which New Labour has turned its back, if it has not rejected it completely.

Yet there is still some cause for optimism. One of those "new social movements" of the 1970s, the Federation of Worker Writers and Community Publishers, still flourishes thirty years later, co-ordinating dozens of local writing and oral history projects across the UK, as well as sustaining a debate (largely overlooked in the literary presses) on the nature of personal and autobiographical writing, on the forms of poetic expression, and on the technicalities of small-scale book production. Several of those idiosyncratic radical bookshops which were so vital to British literary culture in the 1930s — and again in the1970s — still open their doors, and provide a lively base for local literary and cultural life. Centerprise in Hackney, Eastside Books in Stepney, and News from Nowhere in Liverpool, all survive. Within the academy creative writing courses are now *de rigeur*, as is the study of what has become known as "Life-writing". Blogging on the internet has created tens of thousands of new personal narratives, some of which, such as the blog by a young East London paramedic, Tom Reynolds, subsequently published in book version as *Blood, Sweat and Tea: Real Life Adventures in an Inner-City Ambulance*, are every bit as adeptly written and socially concerned as the books discussed here from earlier times.

* * *

In my early months as an English teacher, I was challenged in the classroom one day by a student who, somewhat mischievously, said that since I claimed to know so much about what was good and bad in a piece of writing, how come I hadn't published any poems or novels of my own. No arrow could have pierced more acutely. Since then I have kept my pencils sharpened and a notebook close to hand. Like many others, I cannot imagine a life that does not include writing, not necessarily for publication, but as a way of holding on to it all. Salman Rushdie has written eloquently on this:

> Never forget that writing is as close as we get to keeping a hold on the thousand and one things — childhood, certainties, cities, doubts, dreams, instants, phrases, parents, loves — that go on slipping, like sand, through our fingers.[42]

The Danish writer, Suzanne Brogger, says that writing allows us to step into the same river twice. For this reason, working on a new edition of *Dockers and Detectives* twenty-five years later, I can see that though the political times have changed unimaginably, my original belief that it is through writing that people most convincingly describe the world and make contact with others, still holds true. It allows people to continue a conversation about the ways in which we live now and might perhaps live differently in the future. The world remains a troubled place, yet within it, the part played by the reading and writing of fiction has mostly been a force for the good. It is certainly true that towns and cities are often mythologised into being by writers, often providing their abiding identity. Think of Dickens' London, Joyce's Dublin, Kafka's Prague, or Dideon's Miami. The same happened with London's East End and Liverpool's docklands community, both to the places and the people who inhabited them, and continues to this day, as is evident in the lively controversy surrounding Monica Ali's modern version of East End life, *Brick Lane* (2003). The world is sometimes only as true or real as our descriptions render it.

Looking back on the 1930s, the novelist Sylvia Townsend Warner once wrote that, "we had fought, we had retreated, we were betrayed, and are now misrepresented."[43] That process of misrepresentation of the past is never-ending, and for that reason the proper work of literary evaluation and revaluation is never-ending too. The past is not over, William Faulkner once wrote, it is not even past.

Ken Worpole

[1] While I have genuine admiration for the writing of Iain Sinclair, now regarded as something of a father figure of British psychogeographical writing, some of the themes and obsessions of this school of local and regional history — particularly the obsessive interest in serial killers, gangsters and the underbelly of urban life — in lesser hands has become gratuitous. It has also had the effect of displacing more radical readings of the past as a history of collective struggles and dreams.

[2] The writer Tobias Jones discusses this retreat of idealism — even when wrong-headed — in his fascinating account of contemporary utopian communes in Italy and Britain, *Utopian Dreams*, London, 2007.

[3] Christopher Hilliard, *To Exercise Our Talents: The Democratization of Writing in Britain*, London, 2006, p.132. Hilliard is here citing Andrew Thorpe in the *Historical Journal 43* (2000).

[4] James Vernon, "People's History: Past and Present", presentation at *People's London: In Commemoration of Raphael Samuel*, Conway Hall, London, 2 December 2006.

[5] Christopher Hilliard (2006), *op. cit.*; Jonathan Rose, *The Intellectual Life of the British Working Classes*, London, 2001.

[6] Robert Colls, *Identity of England*, Oxford, 2002, p.341.

[7] Geoff Dench, Kate Gavron & Michael Young, *The New East End*, London, 2006.

[8] Lynsey Hanley, *Estates: An Intimate History*, London, 2007.

[9] Ian Jack, A Very Uncertain Country, *The Guardian*, 10 March 2007, p.3.

[10] A complete run of *Voices* is now available online, thanks to the remarkable efforts of Ken Clay, at www.mancvoices.co.uk

[11] Christopher Hilliard (2006), *op. cit.*, p.258. According to Hilliard, B.L. Coombes, Sid Chaplin and James Hanley all attended and later praised the writing groups they belonged to in

their early careers.

[12]Christopher Hilliard (2006), *op. cit.*, p.50.

[13]In an essay published in *The Guardian* on 11 August 2007, Kelman elaborated upon his dislike of those writers who reserve dialect only for dialogue, and never for the main narration. Reversing this, Kelman often narrates his stories and novels in dialect, but uses Standard English orthography for the dialogue, whether spoken by working-class or middle class characters.

[14]For a detailed and thoughtful study of Kelman's work, see *James Kelman*, by H. Gustav Klaus, London, 2005.

[15]For example, Ferdinand Mount's, *Mind the Gap: Class in Britain Now* (2004), Michael Collins, *The Likes of Us: A Biography of the White Working Class* (2004), Julian Baggini, *Welcome to Everytown: a Journey into the English Mind* (2007).

[16]Reprints of books mentioned in *Dockers & Detectives* and re-published since then include: Simon Blumenfeld's *Jew Boy* (1986) and *Phineas Khan* (1988), Willy Goldman's *East End My Cradle* (1988), James Hanley's *Boy* (1990) and *The Ocean* (1999), Emanuel Litvinoff's *Journey Through a Small Planet* (1993), Dan Billany's *The Cage* (1986), Alexander Baron's *The Lowlife* (2001).

[17]John Williams, "Obituary: Alexander Baron", *The Guardian*, 8 December 1999.

[18]Adam Piette, *Imagination at War: British Fiction and Poetry 1939-1945,* London, 1995.

[19]Raymond Williams, "Double Default", *New Society*, 5 January 1984.

[20]Raymond Williams (1984), *Ibid*.

[21]See especially the chapter on "America in Crisis: 1930-1939" in Barbara Haskell, *The American Century: Art & Culture 1900-1950*, Whitney Museum, 1999.

[22]Christopher Hilliard (2006) *op. cit.*, p.51.

[23]Christopher Hilliard, Ibid. p.52.

[24]Simon Garfield's edited collections from the M-O archives include *Our Hidden Lives* (2004), *We Are At War* (2005) and *Private Battles* (2006). David Kynaston's *Austerity Britain 1945-51*, was published by Bloomsbury in 2007.

[25]See the section "To the West" in Chapter 10 of Jonathan Rose's, *The Intellectual Life of the British Working Classes*, London, 2001, p.353-362.

[26]Ross McKibbin, *Classes and Cultures: England 1918-1951*,

Oxford, 1998.

[27]Richard Ford in interview with Phil Hogan, *The Observer*, 24 September 2006.

[28]Hanley met up with writers such as H.E. Bates, Rhys Davies, T.F. Powys, Liam O'Flaherty, at The Progressive Bookshop in Holborn, run by the German anarchist Charles Lahr and his wife Esther. (John Fordham, *James Hanley: Modernism and the Working Class*, University of Wales Press, 2002, p.93.) Many Jewish writers met and discussed books at the Whitechapel Library under the erudite gaze of a wholly supportive librarian.

[29]Jonathan Rose (2001), p.206.

[30]Arthur R. Taylor, *Labour & Love: An Oral History of the Brass Band Movement*, London, 1983, p.198.

[31]Christopher Hilliard, "Modernism and the Common Writer" in *The Historical Journal 48*, 3, p.769-787, Cambridge, 2005.

[32]Rebecca O'Rourke, "Were there no Women?", *Literature and History*, Vol. 14, No 1, p.48-63. Spring 2005.

[33]Andy Croft, *Red Letters Days: British Fiction in the 1930s*, London, 1990, p.179.

[34]Rebecca O'Rourke (2005), *op. cit.*

[35]Andy Croft (1990), *op. cit.*, p.252.

[36]*Working Lives, Volume I, 1905-45*, London, 1975, *Working Lives, Volume II, 1945-77*, London, 1978.

[37]Rebecca O'Rourke (2005), *op. cit.*

[38]Jenny Hartley, *Millions Like Us: British Women's Fiction of the Second World War*, London, 1997.

[39]See Jenny Hartley, "Letters Were Everything" in Rebecca Earle, ed., *Epistolary Selves: Letters and Letter-Writers 1600-1945*, Aldershot, 1999.

[40]A new edition of letters from the Co-operative Correspondence Club, *Can Any Mother Help Me?* edited by Jenna Bailey, was published by Faber in 2007.

[41]Jenny Hartley (1999), *op. cit.*

[42]Salman Rushdie, Introduction to *Günter Grass: On Writing and Politics*, Harmondsworth, 1987.

[43]This is quoted by Andy Croft (1990), *op. cit.*, p.340.

Fictional Politics:
Traditions and Trajectories

People are not only connected to the past by the historical associations of the material world in which they live. They also inherit intellectual and moral patterns of belief, as well as certain kinds of political and cultural understanding, which though invisible, possess a dogged power of their own to influence their lives. The cluster of traditions surrounding people's relationships to books — to genres of writing and the activity of reading itself — is of enormous cultural power and influence, yet remains largely unexamined.[1] While there are literally thousands of books in print concerning the teaching of reading, less than a handful make any reference whatsoever to the social history of this activity, or to the cultural difficulties that continue to be brought to bear upon the acquisition of this skill. The contemporary reading public and its reading preferences are analysed with regard to book distribution, price, genre, promotion and accessibility; every factor is taken into consideration except possibly the most important one of all, the divided and embattled social history of the activity itself — reading. The history of reading, and the relation between fiction and people's sense of reality and self, remains one of the most interesting cultural questions of the modern world.

Fiction: Unrespectable Writing

The novel in England had its origins in the popular culture of criminal ballads and the street literature of London's underworld or demi-monde. As Lennard J. Davis summarises it in *Factual Fictions: The Origins of the English Novel*:

> The frequency with which the early English novel, newspaper and ballads focused on the criminal is significant.

> There seems to have been something inherently novelistic
> about the criminal, or rather the form of the novel seems
> almost to demand a criminal content. Indeed, without the
> appearance of the whore, the rogue, the cutpurse, the
> cheat, the thief, or the outsider it would be impossible to
> imagine the genre of the novel.[2]

It is not surprising that from the start there should have been prohibitive criticism of the genre, associating the reading of such fiction with a direct criminal influence upon the reader's own behaviour: an early example of the much-debated "transmission effect" in media studies. Davis quotes from many of these early objections, and cites also the defensive or apologetic prefaces written by early novelists assuring the reader that their aim in portraying the criminal underworld was to finally show how such characters all came to an unhappy end or reformed their behaviour. Even so, since the very concept of "fictionality" was then hardly formalised, many early novel-readers assumed that what they were reading was true. And in the formulae used by authors to preface their novels, there was also a suggestion that the writer had simply relayed a story as told to him or her, based on actual events, a framing device which continues in use as for example in the writings of W.G. Sebald.

Until the 1724 Stamp Act, "a turning point in the history of the press and consequently of the novel" according to Lennard, most broadsheet or magazine publications rarely distinguished the factual from the fictional; what are wholly distinct categories of writing for us today were then part of a single literary world. The Stamp Act unintentionally forced publishers to distinguish the two as the Act put a tax on news and left all other forms of writing untaxed. Yet the ambiguity about the reality of what is told in fictional writing, an ambiguity upon which the very form of the novel is predicated, remains with us today, and indeed in post-modern literature has been exploited for particular effect.

This is not simply an effect of the discourse of fiction itself; it is also connected to the phenomenal and almost mesmeric quality of the printed word. Another historian of the early English novel, Ian Watt, wrote that:

> The authority of print — the impression that all that is printed is necessarily true — was established very early. If Autolycus's ballads were in print, Mopsa was "sure they are true". The innkeeper in *Don Quixote* had the same conviction about romances.[3]

In his study *Education and Social Movements*, A.E. Dobbs recounts the story of Stephen Knowles, "a miner dwelling at Grassington... a collector of chap-books, who believed what he read. 'It is not likely,' he argued, 'that anyone would go to the expense of printing lies.'"[4]

This belief could still be found in a fundamental form within popular memory, as was evident in a 20th century South Wales autobiography, *Rhymney Memories* by Thomas Jones:

> ...my father saw in a shop window a book called *The History of Tom Jones* by Henry Fielding. He was intrigued and went in and bought it for eighteen pence vowing he would read it. He never did, as he quickly fell asleep over a long book but my mother read it. She believed every word of it and could not conceive how a man could sit down and invent the story of Squire Allworthy and Sophia and Tom out of his head. So did Robert Owen before her read *Robinson Crusoe* and Richardson's novels and believe every word to be true. But my mother was fifty before she read a novel and to her dying day she had not completely grasped the nature of fiction or drama. The then current attitude is well shown by this sentence from a contemporary lecture by a leading Welsh preacher and Doctor of Divinity: "Novels, the disgrace of English literature, and the curse of multitudes of English readers, do not take with Welsh readers."[5]

The writer was talking about beliefs and attitudes still to be found in the 1920s — some 200 hundred years after the separate discourses of fact and fiction were formally and generically distinguished, demonstrating how resilient such religious and cultural patterns of belief and understanding can be.

The culture of reading was also associated with issues of gender from the beginning. Ian Watt's account of the early novel and its readership details the process by which the new circulating libraries, and the writers themselves, regarded the woman reader as the principal constituent of the reading public. Writing about the first half of the 18th century when the novel was establishing itself as a significant literary form, Watt comments:

> The distribution of leisure in the period supports and amplifies the picture already given of the composition of the reading public; and it also supplies the best evidence available to explain the increasing part in it played by women readers. For, while many of the nobility and gentry continued their cultural regress from the Elizabethan courtier to Arnold's "Barbarians", there was a parallel tendency for literature to become a primarily feminine pursuit.[6]

Another reason for the gender-distribution of the early novel-reading public was that here was a form in which women were early contributors, possibly even founders. In Davis's study of the early novel, he criticises Watt and other historians of the genre for overlooking what was possibly the formative period of the novel before Defoe, to be found in the popular romances of such women writers as Aphra Behn, Mrs Manly, Mary Davys, Eliza Haywood and others.[7]

The gender relationship was simultaneously a class relationship. In the 18th century the novel-reading public was located firmly within the leisured middle and upper classes. As the novel began to separate out into different genres — romantic, picaresque, Gothic, historical — it became much less gender-specific. However, the romantic novel, whose origins in Britain go back conventionally to

Richardson's *Pamela* and thus make it one of the most established of the fictional genres, along with the picaresque novel, has retained a female readership almost exclusively to this day. From its earliest times to the present day, the novel has been one of the few cultural forms in which women have been able to attain a degree of cultural dominance, even though at times they have had to disguise their gender in order to achieve success. This was the case of Mary Ann Evans, most commonly known as George Eliot. There were many others.

A third significant inter-connection has been that of reading with religiosity. "Protestantism," as Halevy once wrote, is a "book religion".[8] In his UNESCO survey of contemporary international publishing, *The Book Revolution*, Robert Escarpit looked back to the first mass movements based on enlarging and capturing the reading public:

> In the last third of the eighteenth century, trends of thought which though at variance with one another, all converged in the direction of spreading books among what was then called "the people" — Methodism in England, Encyclopaedism and later, the revolutionary spirit in France, and, to a lesser extent, *Aufklärung* in Germany — suddenly made the need for reading matter an urgent problem.[9]

Yet there was always a strong distrust — within Nonconformist religions particularly — of imaginative literature. Richard Altick's indispensable study of the 18th and 19th century reading publics summarises this pervasive religious distrust, whilst admitting that the subject deserved a lengthy study in its own right.

> Evangelical denominations possessed a deep suspicion of imaginative literature, a suspicion which fatefully determined the reading experience of millions of people for a very long time. This puritanical proscription — of a literature which did not directly buttress its readers' Christian characters — had a far-reaching an effect upon English culture, with resonances which continue to this day.[10]

Objections were made on a number of grounds. The first was on moral grounds, as it was believed that fictional characters often inhabited a highly secularised world, in which they found happiness or otherwise through material or sensual gratification rather than through piety and self-denial. For the principal narrative ethic which underpinned the romance or the picaresque adventure was, of course, success and achievement in sexual love and material wealth: fictional characters were both in the world and most definitely of it. A second objection was that reading fiction was time-wasting, time that would be better spent on good works, contemplation or direct religious activity.

Such religious objections also carried over into the attitudes of many of the radical working-class movements as well. Richard Carlile, the intrepid and highly energetic 19th century radical publisher and bookseller described himself as "an implacable enemy of all fiction, allegory, personification and romance." Despite many periods of imprisonment during the "war of the unstamped press" in the early part of that century, it does seem likely that given the opportunity Carlile might well have become a quite ruthless censor himself, given his remarks on the popular fiction of the time: "Everything of this kind should now go into the fire. He who burns a romance purifies the human mind."[11]

One can glimpse how both the evangelical and radical distrust affected people deeply by examining the career of one 19th-century working-class radical, George Howell, about whom we have a detailed biography by F.M. Leventhal based on Howell's own letters and reminiscences.[12] Leventhal wrote of Howell's early years of self-education:

> Although familiar with Wordsworth and Byron by this time, Howell continued to avoid Shakespeare until he obtained the reluctant approval of his Methodist class leader, whose suspicion of imaginative literature reflected conventional Evangelical attitudes.[13]

In one of his diary entries — in 1859, while still working as a foreman in the London building trade — Howell describes how he secured a ticket to the British Museum Reading Room, an honour and a privilege he thought would be betrayed by using it to read "any work of fiction or general literature." Moral reservations shade into what was by then an equally censorious utilitarian attitude towards fiction, an attitude less concerned with spiritual dilution than with the fact that imaginative literature produced no direct and measurable benefits to those who read it. Such literature contributed nothing to material progress, unlike works of useful knowledge, encyclopaedias and other forms of self-education and self-improvement. So while Howell was expressing an Evangelical guilt about the reading of fiction, Jeremy Bentham and the utilitarians were also inveighing against such writing which distracted people from the more serious business of the pursuit of happiness.[14]

Ironically, when William Morris came to write his utopian novel *News from Nowhere* a generation later — profoundly anti-utilitarian though he was in most respects — his feelings about fiction echoed those of the utilitarians and the evangelicals. For in the novel, the young woman Clara who represents all that is best in the new socialist commonwealth is shown admonishing her grandfather for his old-fashioned and pre-revolutionary hankering after books to read:

> As for your books, they were well enough for times when intelligent people had but little else in which they could take pleasure and when they must needs supplement the sordid miseries of their own lives with imaginations of the lives of other people. But I say flatly that in spite of all their cleverness and vigour, and capacity for story-telling, there is something loathsome about them. Some of them, indeed, do here and there show some feeling for those whom the history books call "poor", and of the misery of whose lives we have some inkling; but presently they give it up, and towards the end of the story we must be contented to see the hero and heroine living happily in an

island of bliss on other people's troubles; and that after a long series of sham troubles (or mostly sham) of their own making, illustrated by dreary introspective nonsense about their feelings and aspirations, and all the rest of it; while the world must even then have gone on its way, and dug and sewed and baked and built and carpentered round about these useless animals.[15]

That Morris himself had some sympathy with these sentiments, even if he didn't share them entirely, seems likely. The diatribe against "dreary introspective nonsense about their feelings and aspirations" is of a piece with Morris's own antagonism to the modernist literature of his own time, including his particular animus towards the plays of Ibsen. The new concern with exploring the individual psyche and focusing on the more subjective forms of human alienation did not appeal to Morris, in whose own long narrative poems and prose works individual subjective states are pushed aside in the excessive attention to social activity and the emphasis on the physical constraints of life and labour. The notion that mental well-being waited directly upon physical well-being, and that the communism of property would automatically usher in an end to mental distress, was not, in retrospect, a particularly useful contribution to socialist thought.

Traces and echoes of these different attitudes to reading, and particularly the reading of fiction, still exist. In discussions in evening classes, in conversations with librarians and bookshop workers, it is still the case that quite a number of people continue to hold strong reservations about the value, whether moral or utilitarian, of reading fiction — strange though this may seem. Biographies and histories, travel books and documentary books, it is argued by such readers, are far more interesting than fiction and they are "real". Others see reading as a quietist, even anti-social activity. Without an understanding of the complex history of these deeply held attitudes and beliefs, much comments on matters of actual literacy, or patterns of popular reading, particularly non-fiction reading, often end up sounding like a form of Bloomsbury moralism on matters of good and bad taste.[16]

Working-class Reading

One of the great strengths of the British working-class movement was its keen interest in literature and other forms of imaginative writing (principally as an element within a larger concern with self-education). The detailed studies of the 19th century working-class reading public, such as those of Altick, Wickwar, Webb, James, Neuberg and Simons readily attest to this passion.[17] There is Engels' famous passage in *The Condition of the English Working Class* to be remembered:

> I have often heard working-men, whose fustian jackets scarcely hold together, speak upon geological, astronomical, and other subjects, with more knowledge than most "cultivated" bourgeois in Germany possess. And in how great measure the English proletariat has succeeded in attaining an independent education is shown especially by the fact that the epoch-making products of modern philosophical, political, and poetical literature are read by working-men almost exclusively.

One suspects that there was never any great problem in the past about a division between "popular" and "serious" literature and that most people moved easily between the two, as many continue to do today. The early 19th-century radical Samuel Bamford was from an early age intoxicated by the lurid chap-book stories he found for sale in a local printer's shop.[18] In the early part of this century, Glasgow engineering worker and Communist militant, Harry McShane, admitted to an early liking for "bloods". These were "stories about Sweeney Todd and Dick Turpin with people cutting throats and trap-doors and stuff like that."[19] Neither found it difficult to develop more sophisticated tastes or remain eclectic readers throughout their lives.

The rigid demarcation line that separates "popular" and "serious" writing is a product of certain kinds of class

41

attitudes and amplifiers of social distance. Many institutions, particularly the universities, also resisted widening the definition of literature to include a much wider range of popular reading, now realised to have had some important critical value. By erecting high walls around a select number of approved texts, "the canon" as it were, they prevented any possibility of literature being enriched by developments in other genres. Such attitudes also helped stigmatise much other writing, to the extent that many people feel they still have to be apologetic about anything they read that has not been officially approved of as "serious literature".[20]

The division between "serious" and "popular" created a self-fulfilling prophecy and further divided both the literature and its readers into separate camps. (Though at night the dons sometimes went slumming and read great armfuls of detective stories and sometimes wrote them too.) To argue that "literature" is actually an enormously wide body of published (and even unpublished) writing is not to argue that it cannot be discussed, criticised, separated into genres, advocated or condemned, but it is to argue for a pluralism in literary matters — or a continuum — rather than a crude hierarchy or set of discrete and unalterable literary traditions.

Fiction and poetry have also been important vehicles for the exploration of radical ideas. Mary Ashraf's excellent *Introduction to Working Class Literature in Great Britain* details the long history of the fictional representation of radical ideas, from the Chartist novels of Ernest Jones, G.W.M. Reynolds and Thomas Frost and the trade union novels of the 1870s, through to Tressell's *The Ragged Trousered Philanthropists* and the novels of Ethel Carnie prior to the General Strike of 1926.[21] In the 1930s, writers such as Howard Fast and Frank Tilsley succeeded in being both popular and political, but since the Second World War there have been fewer attempts to use fiction as a means of presenting political alternatives, though since the 1970s a number of feminist novels have helped create a strong fictional culture around the ideas and practices of the women's movement.[22]

It is important to recognise too that, contrary to many assumptions, working-class reading patterns were often more adventurous and international in their reach than patterns of middle-class reading. Engels noted this in the 19th century as we have seen, but it was also true in the 20th century. The great interest in the 1930s in American writing, and Russian literature too, was a feature of the reading habits of many working-class radicals, as one see from the autobiographies of that period, as well as through subsequent interviews with members of that generation. In that same period though, a middle-class mass readership was sustained, according to social historians like Claud Cockburn, by stolid English country house detective novels, or romances, in which the only foreigners were either spies, gigolos or mercenary Jews.[23]

Since the war the popularity of such European writers as Camus, De Beauvoir, Sartre, Gunther Grass and Heinrich Böll, and of such American writers as Ray Bradbury, Richard Brautigan, Carson McCullers, Jack Kerouac, Norman Mailer, Henry Miller, William Burroughs, J.D. Salinger and Kurt Vonnegut Jnr., or British writers like Alexander Trocchi, Malcolm Lowry and Michael Moorcock, has usually owed more to rebellious youth movements and sub-cultures, with substantial working-class involvement, than to the literary academy.[24]

Working Class Writing

One of the great difficulties in talking about the many diffuse traditions of working-class writing in Britain is the long shadow cast by Robert Tressell's extraordinary work *The Ragged Trousered Philanthropists*, first published in 1914. For many this one book attained an almost canonical status, to the extent that all other novels about class and politics are compared back to the Tressell novel — and invariably found wanting. Over many years I encountered people for whom the problem of socialist culture would be solved by the arrival of an updated sequel to Tressell's book. Yet it is, of course, the mark of a major cultural achievement — and *The Ragged Trousered Philanthropists* is one — that it cannot be repeated, copied or simply modernised; its singularity is the measure of its achievement.

There was a very rich body of working-class writing in the 19th century, and even earlier, but as much of this work is out of print the prospect of reclaiming and re-evaluating a tradition remains impossible. The only 20th-century collection of Chartist poetry was published in the Soviet Union after the war and became a collector's item in Britain. One particular difficulty in this century is that the "miner's novel" became, after Tressell's book, a new kind of archetypal proletarian fictional model, and other kinds of writing tended to be overlooked. John Field's study of miners as novelists details this tradition up to 1939; in post-war working-class fiction the work of Len Doherty is again most well known, and that again explores the world of the mining community and its political culture.[25] The miner became an archetypal figure of heroic political consciousness in the 20th century.

Yet the 20th century offered an enormous diversity of forms and settings including diaries (two recently published women's diaries, *Nella Last's War* and Diane Harpwood's fictionalised *Tea and Tranquillisers* are important and revealing testimonies for example), childhood evocations, prison writings, experimental novels, short stories, parodies, poems, craft autobiographies, as well as the writings of worker-historians in the History Workshop movement. Though social realism has been the major, though not the exclusive narrative style for fictional work, working-class realism has often been tempered by its own acerbic ironies (some would say bitterness or gallows humour), creating different levels of meaning in different circumstances and conditions of reading. The relationship to the human voice and vernacular speech was often direct and powerful — but also when read aloud open to a variety of ways of interpretation.

The more one explores the many different forms of working-class writing in this century, the more problematic the concepts of "the working-class novel" or "working-class literature" become. Many radical misconceptions have had to be corrected. For what has become a kind of caricature setting for working-class themes in conventional novels (Galsworthy's play *Strike* has much to answer for) — the factory gate, the lock-out, with the work-force being starved back to work — was in no ways dominant in workers' literature itself. The two major traumas that dominate the 20th century novel of working-class life are, not the strike or the factory accident, but unwanted pregnancy and hasty marriage and the back-street abortion.[26] Homelessness and unemployment as other major themes compound and exacerbate the problems of the enforced and unhappy young marriage. Domestic life, rather than working life, was where most of the profound social and psychological pressures were felt.

Popular Literature

Marxist traditions of literary and cultural criticism have often been no more sympathetic to the cultural possibilities of popular literature in this country than have academic criticisms. Moralistic judgementalism — particularly on matters of form — is generic to much radical cultural criticism. In staying so close to selective literary traditions, socialist criticism failed to understand and acknowledge the many new narrative developments and literary registers that popular genre fiction produced. This has been very obviously the case with the radical stylistic originality of American detective fiction, but it is also true of science fiction.

An exception was an essay by Peter Humm on "Reading the lines: television and the new fiction", examining the way in which American novelists like Kurt Vonnegut, Richard Brautigan and Robert Coover emulated the discontinuous narrative forms of television to bring new life and a sense of modernity to popular writing, in a fiction that was also characterised by its social criticism and popular accessibility.[27] These writers have broken down the strict literary divisions between fiction, autobiography and documentary writing by which traditional literary forms have often divided people against their own experience. It also has to be acknowledged that popular literature is often more international and politically wide-ranging in its outlook — think of the work of Len Deighton or John Le Carré for example — than much "serious" literature, which has often been much narrower in its range of geographical, historical and social settings. At one point in the 1960s it was reasonable to ask whether any English novels were being written other than those set in Hampstead or Chelsea.

A fuller understanding of literature has to possess some understanding of the economic and social relationships that inform and underpin the publishing industry. We can never know, in retrospect, what important writing in the past will never became available to us, either because it failed to get published — or quickly disappeared from print never to be seen again. According to the cultural historian Robert Escarpit, "historical selection" causes 80% of literary production to be forgotten within a year and 99% in twenty years.[28] Not all of that work was without historical interest. The interplay between publishing and the book-selling market (and indeed the public library market), is still too little understood. More and more books are published with a pre-planned shelf life of only months, to see if they "take off" or not; otherwise they are withdrawn and pulped.

There will always be "market failure" in the publishing world, because much of it remains producer-led. Poetry cannot be commissioned to order. Thus some kind of public funding for small-scale or experimental initiatives in writing and publishing will always be needed, and thankfully still exists as a matter of public policy in the UK today. In the early 1970s the Swedish government's "Literature Promotion Project" inaugurated a series of books by living working-class writers that were published and sold cheaply on news-stands and in tobacco kiosks throughout Sweden.[29] This was one way of preserving and celebrating a record of local and regional life, culture and history, otherwise likely to be forgotten. In a matter of months these books became "popular literature" in all senses of the phrase — they sold well, and were widely appreciated. Many community publishing initiatives seek to emulate the same ideals, for most literature has its origins in a believable sense of place and its unique web of human relationships.

[1]This has changed remarkably in recent years, as is noted in the new introductory essay to this edition. It was interesting to note that Jonathan Rose's study of working-class culture contained a chapter very similar in theme to this one, "The Difference Between Fact and Fiction", in Jonathan Rose, *The Intellectual Life of the British Working Classes*, London, 2002. There is also much of interest in Franco Moretti's *The Novel, Vol 1: History Geography and Culture, Vol II: Forms and Themes*, London, 2006.

[2]Lennard J. Davis, *Factual Fictions: the Origins of the English Novel*, New York 1983, p125.

[3]Ian Watt, *The Rise of the Novel*, London, 1963, p.205.

[4]A.E. Dobbs, *Education and Social Movements*, London, 1919, p.101.

[5]Thomas Jones, *Rhymney Memories*, Wales, 1970.

[6]Ian Watt (1963), *op. cit.*, p.45.

[7]Lennard J. Davis (1983), *op. cit.*, p.103.

[8]Richard D. Altick, *The English Common Reader*, Chicago, 1957, p.24.

[9]Robert Escarpit, *The Book Revolution*, London, 1966, p.23.

[10]Richard D. Altick (1957), *op. cit.*, p.99.

[11]P.M. Ashraf, *Introduction to Working-class Literature in Great Britain*, Volume 2, Berlin (GDR), 1980, p.13. This volume together with its companion volume on poetry constitutes one of the most thorough histories of working-class literature in Britain in the 18th, 19th and early part of the 20th centuries. It was

never published or distributed in Britain.

[12]F.M.Leventhal, *Respectable Radical: George Howell and Victorian Working-Class Politics*, London, 1971.

[13]F.M.Leventhal (1971), Ibid., p.13.

[14]Richard D. Altick (1957), *op. cit.*, p.133.

[15]William Morris, *News from Nowhere*, in *Three Works by William Morris*, London, 1968, p.337.

[16]Questions of class, snobbery, and attitudes to the popular reading public, are explored in John Carey's book, *The Intellectuals and the Masses: Pride and Prejudiece among the Literary Intelligentsia 1880-1939*, London, 1992.

[17]In for example Altick, *The English Common Reader*, Chicago, 1957; Louis James, *Fiction for the Working Man*, London, 1973; Victor Neuberg, *Popular Literature*, London, 1977; Brian Simons, *Education and the Labour Movement*, London, 1960 and 1965; R.K. Webb, *The British Working-class Reader*, London, 1955 and W. Wickwar, *The Struggle for the Freedom of the Press*, London, 1928.

[18]Victor Neuberg (1977), *op. cit.*, p.113.

[19]Harry McShane and Joan Smith, *No Mean Fighter*, London, 1977.

[20]This has changed remarkably since the first edition of this book, with many universities now making the study of popular literature a key feature of literary studies.

[21]P.M. Ashraf, *Introduction to Working-Class Literature in Great Britain*, Volume 2, Berlin (GDR), 1980.

[22]The novels are too numerous to mention. A number of feminist publishing houses have been started in Britain in recent times, not all remaining, including Virago, The Womens' Press, Onlywomen Press, Sheba Press, Persephone, and others.

[23]See Claud Cockburn, *Bestseller*, London, 1972.

[24]This suggestion remains an intuition. In my own experience, membership of the Labour Party Young Socialists in a provincial town in the late 1950s and early 1960s also meant the circulation of books amongst members by writers such as Camus, Sartre, Kerouac, Mailer and Miller, the City Lights editions of the American Beat poets, and so on. All of this was going on well outside the sphere of influence of the universities or the London literary magazines. The youth culture that formed the milieu for these reading patterns was an increasingly politicised one. This is also the impression given by Jeff Nuttall's *Bomb Culture*,

(London, 1970) though he seems to me to dwell too narrowly on the London scene and the influence of the Art Colleges. American writers like J.D. Salinger, Ray Bradbury and Kurt Vonnegut were read first within the orbit of youth culture — and only later as part of university literary studies. The street was always ahead of the common room. The existence of Penguin books also encouraged the interest of young people in European and American writing in the 1960s. In their classic study of the working-class grammar school pupil, *Education and the Working Class*, Brian Jackson and Dennis Marsden noted how many of the people they interviewed had much of their reading almost "directed" by whatever Penguin published.

[25]John Field, *The Archetypal Proletarian as Author: the Literature of the British Coalfields 1919-1989*, Barnsley, 1981.

[26]This assertion was subsequently challenged by John Lucas in *The Radical Twenties*, Nottingham, 1997, p.158. While he agreed that domestic issues may have dominated working-class fiction in the second half of the 20th century, in the 1920s and early 1930s workplace friction and violence were omnipresent themes, and on this he is probably right.

[27]Peter Humm in P. Widdowson, ed., *Re-Reading English*, London, 1982.

[28]Robert Escarpit (1966), *op. cit.*, p.34.

[29]See Ken Worpole, "Alternative Publishing", *New Society* 3 June 1979.

The American Connection:
The Masculine Style in Popular Fiction

The merits of American style are less numerous than its defects and annoyances, but they are more powerful. It is a fluid language, like Shakespearian English, and easily takes in new words, new meanings for old words, and borrows at will and at ease from the usages of other languages, for example the German free compounding of words and the use of noun or adjective as verb. Its overtones and undertones are not stylised into a social conventional kind of subtlety which is in effect a class language. Final note — out of order. The tone quality of English speech is usually overlooked. This is infinitely variable. The American voice is flat, toneless and tiresome. The English tone quality makes a thinner vocabulary and a more formalised use of language capable of infinite meanings. Its tones of course are read into written speech by association. This makes good English a class language and that is its fatal defect. The English writer is a gentleman first and a writer second.

RAYMOND CHANDLER,
"NOTES ON ENGLISH AND AMERICAN STYLE"

I read H.G. Wells, Arnold Bennett, all those people, but they weren't my kind of people. You always had the edge of class; and what intrigued me about the American writers — of course they had a class system as well — but they were talking the way we talked... What came through with the Americans was really a brutal and realistic attitude in language.

Hemingway was the first because it was his idea that it was in the dialogue that you could do everything, rather than building up descriptive passages... The clarity of the phrase; he was using the vernacular which I liked.

WILLIAM KEAL,
RETIRED TRADE-UNIONIST AND
LABOUR MOVEMENT ACTIVIST[1]

The growth of oral history testifies to the importance now given to popular experience, memory and activity recoverable through personal interviews. Many of these projects have concentrated on experiences of working life, family life, women's work and political activity, the experience of war, trade-union and political membership, alongside childhood recollections and other formative experiences. Less attention has been paid to people's popular cultural experiences: the books they read, the films they saw, the music they listened to, the paintings and posters they remember, and the way in which these aesthetic experiences affected their lives.[2] It is clear that in earlier periods of working-class self-education and political involvement, reading played an important part in widening people's understanding of the world, and that poetry and fiction played a part in highlighting the injustices of the world and the rightness of their cause.

In the twentieth-century, many people in Britain, particularly those active on the left, looked to writers in other countries for forms of literature which addressed more directly the emotional and political experiences which their social class had brought to bear upon their lives. One spur to writing this essay arose out of a conversation I had years ago with an elderly working-class political activist, although the exact circumstances of the discussion have been forgotten. I asked him about the reading habits of his friends when he was younger, and he answered that: "Of course, you must realise, a lot of men were very keen on American paperbacks — detective stories particularly; you wouldn't get them reading novels out of the library."

As a result of this I made a point of asking about early reading patterns and preferences when interviewing older people, and had this assertion confirmed on a number of occasions. The interest in American writing of various kinds was widespread and had important implications for the development of a new style of writing in Britain. On the occasion that I interviewed Jack Dash, the retired rank-and-file dockers' leader, the first writer he

51

mentioned as an important influence was Theodore Dreiser, the founding father of American naturalism. A list of other American writers quickly followed — John Dos Passos, James Farrell, Upton Sinclair — and this register of preferences has been repeatedly invoked by other working-class readers (and sometimes writers) I interviewed over the years.[3]

If the broader "American connection" is obvious, this essay concentrates on one particular genre within the body of twentieth century American writing that made such an impact: the hard-boiled detective novel or "thriller". The study of this particular kind of popular novel raises the question of a symbiotic link between genre writing and mainstream fiction, in which genre fiction is actually in the vanguard of exploring new narrative techniques. Much American crime fiction used vernacular styles of language, more democratically and unselfconsciously, and took fiction into new geographical and social areas of life where the conventional novel was disinclined to go.

This is why the key role of American fiction in the development of a new kind of writing in Britain has to be understood, and why it was the American detective novel in particular that certain writers developed in order to explore Britain's urban and industrial life and culture. The gumshoe (or his British equivalent) went to places where Hercule Poirot had never been. Over time across Europe, the detective novel became one of the most socially critical genres of fiction developed, and is still peering into places and situations that otherwise would remain unexplored. Although it is invidious to make lists in such a wide field, in the novels of Maj Sjöwall and Per Wahlöö, or Henning Mankell in Sweden, Arnaldur Indridason in Iceland, Manuel Vasquez Montalban in Spain, Andrea Camilleri in Italy, Carl Hiaasen and Sara Paretsky in America, or of John Harvey or Ian Rankin in Britain, amongst so many others, we are looking at the work of writers who explore the social and political fractures in their respective societies as profoundly as other, more literary, novelists or social commentators.

The Detective Novel as Genre

The detective novel established itself from the First World War onwards as the most popular form of fiction in European and American culture.[4] Historians of the genre point to William Godwin's *The Adventures of Caleb Williams or Things As They Are* as the first novel to use a murder as the central narrative device. As Godwin's sub-title clearly suggests, the murder itself and its attendant ramifications were an armature around which a political critique of prevailing economic and social relationships could be assembled. The false imprisonment of the main character is used by Godwin as the excuse for a lengthy and bitter attack on despotism, and reads even today as the foundational anarchist text it was meant to be. *Caleb Williams* was published just one year after the same author's dangerously radical *Inquiry into the Principles of Political Justice*. It served to express in fictional form some of Godwin's more direct political sentiments, as well as rehearsing fears concerning his own personal safety, having sown the wind of political rights. The novel is also a story of arbitrary persecution and the adoption of a fugitive life, published in the decade which was to see the establishment of England's first working-class political organisation, the London Corresponding Society — and its rapid suppression.

Such radical origins were somewhat submerged in the late nineteenth and early twentieth centuries as the crime novel became more commonly a vehicle for the upholding of property rights, which wilful murder threatened to overturn or usurp. In Godwin's novel the reader is made well aware that "the law was better adapted for a weapon of tyranny in the hands of the rich, than for a shield to protect the humbler part of the community against their usurpations". There were no doubts here as to where the writer's political sympathies lay.

By the time of the era of the great gentlemen-detectives, however, the genre had become the perfect fictional form for the sacramentality of the executive institutions of the state. Audacious plots to steal the Crown Jewels, rob the Bank of England, poison cabinet ministers, counterfeit the legal tender of the realm, supplant false wills and thus break the ideological continuity of inheritance and primogeniture, issue false share certificates in a deliberate attempt to bankrupt the major companies; all these insidious projects were foiled by the superior minds of gentlemen close to the heart of the establishment (meeting usually in one of the better London Clubs), whose principal task was to ensure the stability and continuity of the English ruling class, at home or abroad.

Yet even these novels could not but reveal (as do most popular genres) some of the political uncertainties and apprehensions of their times. In *One-Way Street*, Walter Benjamin thought that the descriptions in such novels of the ornate settings of the country houses and apartments, rich with tapestries, crowded with heavy dark wooden furniture, exotic ornaments and potted plants, revealed in a way other novels did not, "part of the bourgeois pandemonium."[5] The Italian historian, Carlo Ginzburg, has drawn a detailed analogy between the principles of crime detection postulated by Conan Doyle's master detective, Sherlock Holmes, the near contemporaneous principles of art detection formulated by Giovanni Morelli, and Sigmund Freud's observations on the significance of the accidental and incidental in *The Psychopathology of Everyday Life*.[6] All three "detectives" were developing theories based on the belief that it was in the seemingly insignificant gestures and details of human behaviour that the real clues to the personality were to be found.

The more exotic of the British novels of the period after Sherlock Holmes were adroitly scrutinised by Claud Cockbum in his study, *Bestseller*.[7] Apart from a general glorification of British imperialism, many contained a strong vein of anti-Semitism, often linked with the menace of Bolshevism, together with a portrayal of the working-class as an atavistic mob ever-ready to batter down the park railings. "Consols are down to sixty-five!" is the newspaper headline which marks the full moment of horror in Guy Thorne's *When It Was Dark* (1903). Towards the end of Cockburn's period of study comes Warwick Deeping's immensely popular *Sorrel and Son*, a novel about middle-class failure, partly compensated by the determination to hand something on and thus keep the continuity of inheritance intact:

> Sorrell found his poetry in figures. He was enjoying the romance of hard cash. These glittering sixpences, shillings, florins and halfcrowns, they were the stars above his immediate world, and of far more significance and import than the stars. His means to an end, material plunder for immaterial needs. For with his savings he was going to arm his son against a world that babbled of socialism but still clutched a knife or a club... Only the indispensable and the individual few would be able to rise above the scramble of the industrial masses. It is the few who matter and who will always matter. So Sorrel thought.

In the 1920s and 1930s the crime novel dealt with many of the same fears as the earlier novels, but less exotically. The detective novel in this period was a form of fictional reassurance for a middle-class readership that the continuity of the existing social order was safe. Few detective novels in this period were based in the industrial or commercial cities, thus avoiding having to acknowledge the existence of an urban working-class. Rather they were set, in the words of another critic of the genre, "in a village, largely a commuters' village in the Home Counties where there's a church, a village inn, very handy for the odd Scotland Yard inspector and his man who come to stay for the regularly recurring crimes..."[8] Such working-class people who appeared in these novels did so as quasi-feudal retainers: cooks, butlers, domestic servants, gardeners and sometimes a local policeman who often exemplified a particular kind of "rural idiocy".

Writing his "Bookshop Memories" in November 1936, George Orwell thought that the divide in popular fiction between "the average novel — the ordinary, good-bad, Galsworthy-and-water stuff which is the norm of the English novel" and the detective novel was exclusively along gender lines: women reading the former and men the latter.[9] This contrasts with the opinions of other commentators who have often assumed the readership of the country house murder to be mostly women. Uncharacteristically, Orwell failed to mention class tastes in this short impressionistic account of the reading public based on his own bookshop experiences. Elsewhere he deprecates the American private-eye novels of James Hadley Chase, finding them sadistic and lawless, suggesting that the American dime novel had already arrived. By the mid 1930s it was American writers who were beginning to find a wide readership in Britain, often among working-class men — a shift which by the late 1940s had become a significant cultural fact. For while they espoused a degree of violence and sexual aggression, these writers portrayed the life of the back-streets, bars, and big business dealings at the heart of political corruption, of which their English counterparts appeared completely innocent.

In *The Uses of Literacy* (1957) Richard Hoggart was keenly aware of this turn towards a genre developed in another country with quite different social and cultural histories. He regarded the American tough-guy novel as an undifferentiated type, read, he thought, for its sexual content above all. By only highlighting such writers as James M. Cain and Mickey Spillane, he failed to signal some rather more intriguing aspects of the attraction of the American detective novel for British readers. Though correct to see that the prose style itself was something new — vernacular, terse, rather tough — in describing it as "debased Hemingway" he failed to consider that Hemingway's style itself had developed from the hard-boiled school of thriller writing, and indeed could not be critically separated from it. Hoggart was right, however, in appreciating that because these novels were sited in the life of the "megalopolis", they were attractive to the British working-class reader, for whom the Edwardian country-house murder was remote in both space and time.

American writing became even more firmly established in Britain after the Second World War. As John Sutherland noted:

> War stifled film-going and dining-out and had the paradoxical effect of stimulating reading while inhibiting the production of new books... People wanted fiction, and less was being produced. One consequence was the spectacular boom in American novels. Selling American rights was suddenly as easy as "falling off a log", an agent, Juliet O'Hea, recalled.[10]

Thus it was that in American fiction many British working-class readers found a realism about city life, an acknowledgement of big business corruption, and an unpatronising portrayal of working-class experience and speech still not found in British popular fiction of the period — least of all in the English murder story, obsessed as it was with the corpse in the library, the Colonel's shares on the stock market and thwarted passion on the Nile.

American Naturalism

Of the many ways of understanding how literature reflects the society in which it is produced, the study of genres is particularly useful in trying to understand what makes popular literature popular. The development of a genre is the development of a series of internal rules, narrative templates and social understandings which make the structure of a cultural form at once familiar, recognisable and accessible. Developments in popular culture are necessarily developments within popular genres. Russian formalist criticism — in the writings of theorists like Shklovsky — asserted that many achievements in literature arise through "the canonisation of inferior (sub-literary) genres"; that in effect Dostoevsky's novels were in essence crime novels, Pushkin's lyrics a refinement of "album verses", and so on.[11] What great writers do is take popular forms and give them new layers of depth and meaning.

However, to write genre fiction is to risk losing critical acceptance and approval, although the rewards of cultural influence through a wider readership are potentially much higher. This is why it has become a commonplace to credit Hemingway with the development of a terse, unsentimental style of writing which gave such a fillip to the development of American vernacular writing, even though it is likely that Hemingway took his lessons from the early short-story writing of dime magazine writer Dashiell Hammett. This is certainly the opinion of Julian Symons:

> People say sometimes that perhaps Hammett was influenced by Ernest Hemingway but in fact any influence there may have been was the other way round because Hammett had started writing his stories in the early 1920s: the first one appeared in 1921 well before Hemingway had started writing.[12]

While French writers such as Camus and Sartre publicly admired the developments in technique which Hammett particularly brought to the novel — in terms of its passionless, anonymous narrator and its milieu of cheap hotels, boarding houses, bars and cynical sexual alliances — orthodox literary opinion in Britain ignored the work of Hammett and other American detective novel writers as beneath attention. Camus himself admitted that if it had not been for reading James M. Cain's *The Postman Always Rings Twice* he would not have had the idea and psychological structure for *L'Etranger*, one of the most celebrated post-war European novels.[13] Other American writers in the detective genre were greatly admired in France. Horace McCoy, author of *They Shoot Horses, Don't They?* and *No Pockets in a Shroud* was described in the late 1930s as "the most discussed American writer in

France", admired for the "objective lyricism" of his narrative style."[14]

British novelists, in contrast, resisted the modernising developments in narration and style developed in other countries as well as in genre writing, as if nothing had changed radically since Galsworthy. The insularity of British fiction continued to be celebrated by its practitioners, and experimentalism in writing was seen to be the preserve of eccentrics (Christine Brooke-Rose, B.S. Johnson) or foreigners (Nathalie Sarraute, Thomas Bernhard). This is evident in remarks made by Kingsley Amis on the state of British fiction in the 1970s:

> I think that one of the reasons why, according to me, the English novel has got it over the American novel at the moment is because of things like English snobbery, and English conservatism and English class consciousness and all that kind of thing. Because I think that all this so-called wave of modernism has hit the English novel less hard than any other kind of novel. It seems to me that, little as I know of it, thank God, the French novel is in smithereens now, because of that wave.[15]

Making allowances for Amis's consistent liking for parody, there is a large degree of truth represented in these remarks. Even when socially minded writers in Britain have chosen to write genre fiction — for example G.D.H. and Margaret Cole jointly wrote detective novels, as did C. Day Lewis and Christopher Caudwell among others — they failed to use the genre as a medium for any accompanying radical developments in technique or ideas. No wonder that so many working-class readers, particularly men, found American writing so much more accessible in style and subject matter in comparison to the classical formalism of the English novel of suburban manners — and murders.

The great popular early masterpiece of American naturalism was Theodore Dreiser's *An American Tragedy*, published in 1925. Dreiser himself had been brought up in bitter poverty in one of the mill-towns of Indiana and became a journalist on leaving school. That so many American writers started out as journalists — Dreiser, Hemingway, Chandler, all did so — exemplifies a quite different route to writing than that followed by most English writers at the time, who were much more likely to be public school graduates with a private income and connections to the major publishing houses. Dreiser's writing was immensely detailed in its descriptions of place and circumstance: H.L. Mencken wrote in an introduction to one edition of *The American Tragedy* that if a train timetable was given in a Dreiser novel it was guaranteed to be right, and that every street scene in every novel had its exact original in some American town or city. Dreiser's sympathies were with the American common people, despite their faults, and he wrote about them unpatronisingly and with considerable insight and care. It is difficult to imagine a work of popular fiction published in Britain at this time (1925) in which working-class people would be portrayed realistically, let alone sympathetically.

Dreiser's novel was based on a real murder in 1906, when a young man drowned his pregnant girlfriend and was executed for his crime. In Dreiser's version, the young man plans such a murder, but when the time comes to carry this out cannot go through with it. However, by accident the girl does drown and because of a mass of circumstantial evidence as to the young man's intentions he is tried for murder, found guilty and executed. This device was also adopted by James M. Cain in *The Postman Always Rings Twice*, wherein someone is condemned for the intention rather than the act. This was the irony much admired by Camus. Thus the plot could hardly be more simple; the power and interest lay in the way in which it described the lives and values of American urban life, the ambitions and corruption, the dreams of success set against the miseries of slum life and the experience of prison.

By the time *An American Tragedy* was published, both Hammett and Hemingway had short stories in print.

Hammett had his first work published in 1921, and Hemingway's small collection of "fragments", *In Our Time*, came out in 1923. All argument about who actually influenced whom remains speculation; however the connection between the two is not in doubt. Both had developed their writing through their work: in Hemingway's case as a reporter and in Hammett's as a Pinkerton detective. Hemingway acknowledged the influence of the style-sheets of the *Kansas City Star* with their instructions to "avoid the use of adjectives, especially such extravagant ones as splendid, gorgeous, grand, magnificent". Hemingway later recalled that these were, "The best rules I ever learned for the business of writing." There was also the discipline involved in transmitting stories by transatlantic cable which put an economic premium on each word. Hammett's early writing had consisted of case reports about his work at the detective agency which in later life Hammett recalled for their "literary quality".

As has been noted, in Julian Symons' opinion, Hammett was the true pioneer in the development of the austere vernacular style so much admired in Hemingway. Andre Malraux thought the same, commenting in 1937 that Hammett was the "technical link" between Dreiser and Hemingway.[16] The question is important because it is usually considered the case that Hemingway's distinctive style can be attributed in part to the influence of Pound and Gertrude Stein in Paris. Yet it may well be that he owed as much, if not more, to the developments achieved by Dashiell Hammett in his dime magazine stories: a rather less exotic parentage but one which at least acknowledges the modernising pressures of popular taste.

There were more direct material pressures which also helped to produce this condensed style of writing. Of the twenty-five stories Hammett had published between November 1922 and June 1924, half were less than 2,500 words. Hemingway's first collection, *In Our Time*, is simply a collection of short sketches, some less than one hundred words in length. Neither Hammett nor Hemingway began by regarding themselves as apprentice novelists, but rather as people who wanted to use writing as sharply and clearly as possible to describe an incident, recreate a conversation, portray violence and fear as curtly as was possible. Both cultivated a prose style that had the appearance of objective reporting. As Hemingway said about his own writing:

> The test of a book is how much good stuff you can throw away. I use the oldest words in the English language when I write. People think I'm an ignoramus who doesn't know the ten-dollar words. I know the ten-dollar words. But there are older, better words....[17]

Hammett narrated nearly all his short stories and early novels between 1923 and 1930 in the words of his anonymous private investigator working for the Continental Detective Agency, using the vocabulary of a gumshoe rather than the distanced syntax of an omniscient narrator. Chandler, when writing about the importance of Hammett in establishing the genre of the "hard-boiled" American detective novel, pointed out how Hammett's radical literary break-through arose out of his exactness of ear for popular speech:

> He had a literary style, but his audience didn't know it, because it was in a language not supposed to be capable of such refinements. They thought they were getting a good meaty melodrama written in the kind of lingo they imagined they spoke themselves. It was, in a sense, but it was much more. All language begins with speech, and the speech of common men at that, but when it develops to the point of becoming a literary medium it only looks like speech.[18]

With the extensive use of the vernacular, particularly in Hemingway's second collection, significantly titled *Men Without Women* (1927), came the now familiar "Hemingway" narrative syntax, based on successive short, lapidary sentences.

The Emergence of a "Masculine" Style

This new development in narrative style was always described in terms of its masculinity, in the critical reception of both writers. Of *The Maltese Falcon*, one reviewer thought Hammett's writing "better than Hemingway; since it conceals not softness but hardness". Another reviewer of the same novel referred to "the sheer force of Hammett's hard, brittle writing (which) lifts the book out of the general run of crime spasms and places it aloof and alone as a brave chronicle of a hard-boiled man, unscrupulous, conscience-less, unique." The prose of Hemingway's first collection, *In Our Time*, is described as being made up of,

> ...stubby verbal forms speeded in instances up to the brute, rapid, joyous jab of blunt period upon period. Hemingway's vocabulary is largely monosyllabic, and mechanical and concrete... Hemingway's style... in its very experimental stage shows the outline of a new, tough, severe and satisfying beauty related equally to the world of machines and the austerity of the red man.[21]

The subsequent collection was reviewed by Cyril Connolly in *The New Statesman* thus:

> *Men Without Women* is a collection of grim little stories told in admirable colloquial dialogue with no point, no moral and no ornamentation. They are about bull-fighters, crooks, crook prize-fighters, crook peasants, dope fiends and soldiers in hospital. The title is intended to strike the note of ferocious virility which characterises the book, which is, however, by no means free from the strong silent sentimentality latent in this attitude.[20]

These stories were the precursors of was what later to develop anew in the 1970s and 1980s as American "dirty realism", a label most commonly associated with the gifted short story writer, Raymond Carver, and, to a lesser extent, the novelist Richard Ford.

The belief that there are distinct "masculine" and "feminine" styles of writing is not new, though it doesn't really surface in the apparatus of criticism until after the First World War, with the break-up of traditional narrative forms under the impact of modernism. Until then, as a university subject English Literature itself was considered a "feminine" subject until the appearance of "scientific" (i.e. masculine) linguistic criticism, developed by I.A. Richards in the 1920s. Historically the novel was the one cultural form in which women earned for themselves an equal, if not superior, status to that of men. Thus a noted authority on style in this period, Sir Arthur Quiller-Couch, could point out some of the gender-inflected attributes of writing:

> Generally use transitive verbs, that strike their objects and use them in the active voice, eschewing the stationary passive, with its little auxiliary is's and was's, and its participles getting in the light of your adjectives, which should be few. For, as a rough law, by his use of the straight verb and by economy of adjectives, you can tell a man's style, if it be masculine or neuter, writing or composition.[21]

The narrative styles of Hemingway and Hammett are clear examples of this renunciation of all detail other than action, dialogue and a minimal description of place-setting. No characters ever have their thoughts articulated; what we know about their inner lives has to be inferred from their speech and their behaviour. The omnipotent, all-seeing narrator of conventional narrative discourse has been dispensed with, and one can argue that the "dime novel" arrived at this advance post of fictional development several decades ahead of the *nouveau roman*.

In between the first edition of one of the sketches from *In Our Time* and the revised edition published eight years later,

> Hemingway reduced the 241 words to 121, the more than thirty descriptive adjectives to ten, shortened the length of the sentences, changed some of the adjectives to past participles, added several present participles, and made all the sentences simple and declarative[22]

Nothing remotely similar to this modernising, relentless paring down of style was happening at this time in English fiction. This is why when Chandler (who had been educated in England at Dulwich College) started to write, following in the style of Hammett, he stated that,

> I had to learn American just like a foreign language... Thank heaven that when I tried to write fiction I had the sense to do it in a language that was not all steamed up with rhetoric.[23]

This concern with objectifying the language of the novel was one which accounted for the French enthusiasm for the "hard-boiled" American detective novel, an appreciation of style which was part of a reciprocal admiration between French and American writers. It was, after all, one of the most famous maxims of Voltaire that "the adjective is the enemy of the verb". Flaubert's perfectionism was the standard by which a number of American writers at this time judged themselves. In Hemingway's *Green Hills of Africa* the narrator tells Kandinsky that one of the most important things for a writer to have is "the discipline of Flaubert". In writing to his publisher, Hamish Hamilton, in 1949, Chandler listed the eight stories in European literature he most admired as "all perfect": three were by Flaubert.

Both Hemingway and Chandler thought American English to be much more open to modern experience than the formalism of the language they found among the English upper classes they met in London or in Paris. One of Hemingway's first published miniatures for *In Our Time* was a parody of an English officer's speech: "It was a frightfully hot day. We'd jammed an absolutely perfect barricade across the bridge. It was simply priceless..." In a number of his novels, characters are often to be found commenting sarcastically on formal English speech. In *The Sun Also Rises*, Jake Barnes remarks that "When you are with the English, you get into the habit of using

English expressions in your thinking. The English spoken language, the upper classes', anyway, must have fewer words than the Eskimo." In Chandler's essay comparing the two styles of language, he thought American English,

> ...emotional and sensational rather than intellectual. It expresses things experienced rather than ideas... Why then can it produce great writing or at any rate writing as great as this age is likely to produce? The answer is, all the best American writing has been done by men who are, or at some time were, cosmopolitans. They found here a certain freedom of expression, a certain richness of vocabulary, a certain wideness of interest... compared with it at its best, English has reached the Alexandrian stage of formalism and decay.[24]

Several critics in England at this time recognised the problem of the opaqueness and self-aggrandisement of English narrative style. In 1931 the English poet and art critic (and philosophical anarchist) Herbert Read published his detailed analysis of *English Prose Style*. In separating out the various structural and linguistic elements which combine to form "prose style", he pointed to a proper interest in narrative as being the most distinctive weakness of English writing:

> ...good narrative writing is comparatively rare in English literature. There is a human failing which urges us to elaborate and decorate our descriptions; it is perhaps merely the desire to infuse an objective activity with something of the personality of the narrator.[25]

Although there is a tradition of narrative simplicity in English fiction, and a speed and economy in relating a story, found in Defoe, Bunyan, and the picaresque novel, there is another tradition which came to be favoured. Here the novel became a rhetorical form, in which detailed description of place, custom and dress, together with an appropriate amount of moral reflection, tended to weigh down the progress of the narrative to a debilitating degree.

The enormous effort — articulated most explicitly by Matthew Arnold — to make English literature a substitute for religion, a new moral currency of culture, gave the novel a greater sense of its own importance, but at the expense, some might say, of its story-telling, democratic obligations. As Read himself noted of the pre-novel literary forms: "In the older forms of narrative, such as the Fable, the Allegory, and the Parable, the action is coherent and unimpeded."[26] The novel, though, in its development within English culture, has often almost tried to dispense with action altogether. This does go some way towards explaining that massive disjunction in this century between the novel of manners and the popular novel of action and narrative speed.

The Influence of Hammett and Hemingway

Between them, Hammett and Hemingway developed a tough, masculine, vernacular (or demotic) style of writing which helped transform and democratise American literature from the 1930s onwards, and which provided a vicarious excitement and a sense of freedom for a number of British readers, for whom the English short story and novel were still perceived to be preoccupied with the minutiae of domestic morals and manners. By contrast, Hammett and Hemingway evoked a harsh (but definitely twentieth-century) world of mining towns, transit camps, life on the road, seedy bars, boxing rings, corrupt city governments, and a proletarian politics that took guns and baseball bats to picket lines. At the centre of these stories were the stoical men who recorded everything they saw, who tried to retain some basic decency, tried to put things straight and restore a sense of order: Hemingway's Nick Adams; Hammett's anonymous agency detective who finally, in *The Maltese Falcon*, becomes the mythical Sam Spade. Such characters were quintessentially the "degraded" heroes (Barthes) engaged in a "demoniacal" (Lukacs) search for authentic values of the twentieth-century European novel, but they achieved a reading public far beyond that of the erstwhile literary novel.

In Hammett's hands, the detective novel became a vehicle for radical social criticism, without reading like a polemical text. In Hammett's work police, politicians and big business invariably combine together to run the city administration in their own interests, even though this often involves murder, gang-slayings, bribery and perjury. The scale of civic corruption in *Red Harvest* and *The Glass Key* is extraordinary, yet it is cleverly treated as a backcloth, or night-town milieu, in which the detective works in response to other interests. The jungle of the cities which Brecht wanted to portray to European theatre audiences, Hammett had already fictionalised for his dime magazine readers. Brecht's *City of Mahagonny* (1929) is directly related to Hammett's "Poisonville" in *The Red Harvest* of the same year, sharing a common setting, imagery and *dramatis personae*. Wim Wenders's film *Hammett* (1982) acknowledged that shared understanding in the garish expressionism of his Chinatown and waterfront settings.

Yet as well as the economic and political corruption evident in these novels, which are conventions of the "hard-boiled" school of writing, there is also sexual corruption and even a degree of sadism too.[27] The women always play an obstructive role, threatening to emasculate or betray the stoical heroes on their lonely journeys through the mean streets, on the adolescent camping expeditions, or during the final shoot-out which brings the typical detective novel to its end. Women do not figure as strong characters — let alone moral agents — in Hemingway's work. The early Nick Adams stories are about the painful decision to break off the relationship with Marjorie and its choice of a single life of action and self-discovery; in *A Farewelll to Arms*, the woman dies on the last page, leaving the man to walk off into the night, alone, in the rain.

In the novels of Hammett and Chandler this ending is developed into an established convention of the genre. In

Hammett's *Red Harvest* the principal woman character and potential lover of the detective is murdered two-thirds of the way through the book; in *The Dain Curse* the central female figure is saved from heroin addiction by the detective, but when she makes a sexual advance towards him is rejected; in *The Maltese Falcon* the same *femme fatale* is handed over to the police at the end, even though Sam Spade loves her; and in *The Glass Key* the detective does leave at the end with a woman to travel to another city, but it is an arrangement of convenience and made without any emotional commitment.

In Chandler's novels the misogyny becomes more extreme. One Chandler critic, Michael Mason, points to the increasingly obvious development in the novels of Marlowe's own homosexual inclinations, made more pronounced by the growing distaste for women evident in the writing.[28] The "tough guy" novel is, in fact, predicated on a deep ambiguity about sexual identity. In a collection of "Casual Notes on the Mystery Novel" (1949) Chandler seemed to be rationalising a state of affairs with regard to his own detective creation, Marlowe, when he renounced the possibility of any kind of achieved and settled sexual relationship for the detective in the mystery novel:

> The only effective kind of love interest is that which creates a personal hazard for the detective — but which, at the same time, you instinctively feel to be a mere episode. A really good detective never gets married.[29]

Chandler's own writing, based as it was originally on admiration for Hammett and Hemingway, whom he often cited, became increasingly sophisticated and moved away from the popular and demotic. The descriptions of the settings became longer, although they were always characterised by a mordant and acerbic irony. The similes piled on top of each other, the dialogue became more consciously dry-witted and more often self-consciously studded with intellectual and literary allusions, the perorations on human weakness, civic corruption and sexual infidelity became longer. The cost of refining the genre was that it began to look towards a different readership for approval as it became more self-consciously literary and settled back again into conventional narrative forms.

The one thing that Chandler continued to share with the earlier "tough-guy" writers was a hatred of police corruption and police brutality. In his last complete novel, *The Long Goodbye*, the portrait of the police is savage. The one honest police officer in the novel is described to his face by Marlowe as talking "like a Red". "I wouldn't know," the office replies, "I ain't been investigated yet." This was written in the early period of McCarthyism. Elsewhere in the novel a character tells Marlowe, "That's the difference between crime and business. For business you gotta have capital. Sometimes I think it's the only difference."

It was for such sentiments that the "tough-guy" novel came under rearguard attack from one of America's most distinguished cultural critics, Jacques Barzun, who defended the "ethical, civilised, and in the best sense literary" qualities of the classic detective genre, against the "pseudo-realism" and "nihilistic vandalism" of Hammett and Chandler, noting, with not a little dash of red-baiting, that "the tough story was born in the thirties and shows the Marxist colouring of its birth years."[30] Condemned by the literary establishment in America for its sordid milieux and the cynical (but dangerously radical) eye cast on the widespread existence of political corruption, it was also denounced by Communist aestheticians in the same period. Many derogatory references were made to the detective novel during the course of the Soviet Writers' Congress of 1934, of which Zhdanov's was most scathing: "The 'illustrious persons' of bourgeois literature — of that bourgeois literature which has sold its pen to capital — are now thieves, police sleuths, prostitutes, hooligans."[31]

Chandler's influence on the British reading public was considerable, and he often remarked that his work enjoyed a more enthusiastic reception in Britain than in America. A year before his death, while staying in London, he read an extract of an autobiographical novel by Frank Norman in *Encounter* magazine. Frank Norman was an orphan brought up in a Dr Barnardo's Home and sent to prison at an early age on a robbery charge. His prison memoir, *Bang to Rights*, published in 1958, was an important contribution to the new wave of working-class realism which broke across British culture in the late 1950s and early 1960s. Having read the *Encounter* extract, Chandler offered to write a foreword: "There is no damned literary nonsense about his writing. Frank Norman writes swiftly and closely about things... An observation so sharp should not be lost to the world. We need it. He has it."[32]

In the same year, Brendan Behan's *Borstal Boy* was published, as was Alan Sillitoe's *Saturday Night and Sunday Morning*. Neither Behan, Sillitoe, Bernard Kops, Bill Naughton and the other first-generation writers who emerged in that period chose to write genre fiction; they wrote prison autobiographies, childhood memoirs (to which Keith Waterhouse and Leslie Thomas contributed two fine books), or short stories and novels based on modern working-class picaresque heroes: Sillitoe's Arthur Seaton, Bill Naughton's Alfie. Yet the great narrative and stylistic caesura which separates their writing from that of socialist novelists of the pre-war period, such as Howard Fast and Frank Tilsley, for example, could not have been resolved in British writing without the direct influence of the American realist tradition. By the 1940s and 1950s, other American writers like Steinbeck and Salinger were being avidly read in Britain, and their crisp, popular colloquial style was widely admired and emulated.

What continues to be obvious, is that the "tough-guy", vernacular style of writing, was often adopted by many British working-class male writers as the appropriate register for writing about their experiences. The settings are frequently detached from routine daily life (including the workplace) and are often exclusively male: betting shops, pubs, cafes. Family life is rarely dealt with in great detail. From Sillitoe's quick-tongued, go-down-fighting, working-class rebels, via Bill Naughton's eponymous Alfie and Alan Bleasedale's Franny Scully, the narration — often in first person — is of a piece with that developed by American realism.

No one can doubt the strengths of this style — its celebration of individual resistance to arbitrary authority, its quick-witted repartee, the emphasis on the moral autonomy of the narrator or main character. Yet there were disadvantages too. The most obvious was the failure to engage with the detail of personal and domestic relationships. The ideological roots of this persona combine a mixture of Protestant individualism with a dash of iron-in-the-soul existentialism. Its material basis was to be found in the relative autonomy which men possessed within the work-place and the urban street, compared with that of women. The world in which the vernacular flourished was that city life in which the semi-independent, entrepreneurial working-class was to be found: in the street markets, among cab and lorry drivers, in the casualised world of the building trade, and of course among those involved in crime.

[1]This comment was made during an interview by Ken Worpole with William Keal in early 1983.

[2]Since this was written, the lengthy studies by Christopher Hilliard (2006) and Jonathan Rose (2001) have added enormously to our understanding of popular reading and writing interests over the past hundred years.

[3]Interview by Ken Worpole with Jack Dash, 15 June 1982.

[4]See Julian Symons, *Bloody Murder: From the Detective Story to the Crime Novel*, Harmondsworth, 1974.

[5]Walter Benjamin, *One-Way Street and Other Writings*, London, 1974, p.49.

[6]Carlo Ginzburg, "Morelli, Freud and Sherlock Holmes: Clues and the Scientific Method", *History Workshop Journal 9*, London, 1980.

[7]Claud Cockburn, *Bestseller: The Books That Everyone Read 1900-1939*, London, 1972.

[8]Colin Watson, *Crime Writers*, London, 1978, p.61.

[9]George Orwell, *Essays, Journalism and Letters*, Vol.1, Harmondsworth, 1970, p.275.

[10]John Sutherland, *Fiction and the Fiction Industry*, London, 1978, p.3.

[11]See Rene Wellek and Austin Warren, *Theory of Literature*, Harmondsworth, 1973, p.235.

[12]From the BBC programme notes for the series *Crime Writers*, London,1978.

[13]See W.M. Frohock, *The Novel of Violence in America*, New York, 1950.

[14]See D. Madden, ed., *Tough-Guy Writers of the Thirties*, New York, 1968.

[15]Sutherland (1978), *op. cit.*, p.22.

[16]Richard Hayman, *Shadow Man: The Life of Dashiell Hammett*, London, 1981.

[17]Dennis Pepper ed., *A Hemingway Selection*, London, 1977, p.195. This anthology, which includes early reviews of Hemingway's work along with most of his well-known short stories was an edition for schools, a reminder of how important American writing — Hemingway, Steinbeck, Salinger and so on — had been in the curriculum of British schools as a source of vivid narrative writing free of the class sentiment which distinguishes English writers of the same period.

[18]D. Gardiner and K. Sorley Walker eds, *Raymond Chandler Speaking*, London, 1962.

[19]Dennis Pepper (1977), *op. cit.*, p.183.

[20]Dennis Pepper (1977), *op. cit.*, p.184.

[21]Sir Arthur Quiller-Crouch, *The Art of Writing*, London, 1916, p.23. Yet in this period, significantly, Dorothy Richardson was, in the words of Virginia Woolf, developing something she consciously described as a "women's sentence". Gillian Hanscambe's study of Richardson (*The Art of Life*, London, 1983) makes this question of a feminist style of writing a central theme and quotes Virginia Woolf's taxonomy of what such a syntax involves: "a sentence of a more elastic fibre than the old, capable of stretching to the extreme, of suspending the frailest particles, of enveloping the vaguest shapes" (p.40). Syntactic structures, then, are not merely questions of aesthetics but reflect class and

gender attributes as well.

[22]L.W. Wagner ed. *Ernest Hemingway: Five Decades of Criticism*, Ann Arbor, 1974, p.14.

[23]Frank MacShane, *The Life of Raymond Chandler*, London, 1976, p.48.

[24]Frank MacShane (1976), *op. cit.*, p.81.

[25]Herbert Read, *English Prose Style*, London, 1931, p.105.

[26]Herbert Read (1931), Ibid.

[27]It was the sadistic, misogynistic streak in American crime fiction that Orwell and later Hoggart most objected to, though this was also found in British imperial/spy fiction of the same period, though more obliquely. It re-emerged with a vengeance in the novels of Ian Fleming.

[28]In Miriam Cross, ed., *The World of Raymond Chandler*, London, 1972.

[29]Miriam Cross (1972), *op. cit.*, p.70.

[30]Jacques Barzun and W.H. Taylor, *Catalogue of Crime*, New York, 1971.

[31]*Soviet Writers Congress 1984*, London, 1977, p.90.

[32]Frank MacShane, *The Life of Raymond Chandler*, London, 1976, p.261.

The Popular Literature
of the Second World War

It is commonly claimed that the Second World War, unlike the First, produced no significant body of literature in English. The poetry of Julian Grenfell, Ivor Gurney, Rupert Brooke, Edward Thomas, Isaac Rosenberg, Wilfrid Owen and Sigfried Sassoon, together with such memorable works as Edmund Blunden's *Undertones of War*, Robert Graves's *Goodbye To All That* and Vera Brittain's *Testament of Experience*, are cited as constituting a profound range of imaginative writing that embodied the terrible loss and enormity of "The Great War". Very little work of the same intensity, it has been argued, emerged from the Second World War, though the achievements of Sidney Keyes, Alun Lewis, Keith Douglas, Hamish Henderson and Henry Reed in poetry are mentioned as constituting a small qualification that prevents the complete dismissal of the literature of the 1939-1945 period entirely.[1]

Within the limits of what is defined as literature by the "selective tradition", this may well be true. Critical works about this period, such as *The Penguin Guide to English Literature: The Modern Age* (1961), Robert Hewison's *Under Siege* (1979), Walter Allen's *Tradition and Dream* (1964) and Ronald Blythe's anthology *Components of the Scene* (1966), place too much emphasis on received notions of literature, and not enough on writing.[2] The result is that an enormous body of writing about the Second World War — such as escape stories, concentration camp memoirs, resistance novels and autobiographies of ordinary combatants — was ignored. This is particularly noticeable in Blythe's anthology, subtitled "An anthology of the prose and poetry of the Second World War", which contains not one piece of documentary writing, nor any account of life in the prison and concentration camps, nor any writing by or about life in "the other ranks". The cultural myopia of English literary criticism could not be more evident. The great wall which separates "literature" from "writing", then as now, creates more cultural problems than it solves. The so-called canon has proved blind to engaging with the greater body of writing which came out of the war, as most of it came in forms — letters, diaries, memoirs, stories — which were deemed to be of no enduring value.

The "selective tradition" makes critical life easier at an academic level, for there are certainly many less books to read, fewer silences to register, or narrative forms to acknowledge and genres to accommodate. But critical work ought not to be easy, because it could be the case that popular literature actually requires more critical attention and understanding than the canon, rather than less.

The most widely read books in Britain in the 1950s were those that dealt with the experiences of male combatants in the Second World War, a fact which literary histories have barely acknowledged. Women's experiences of the Second World War were largely ignored in this period, except for translations of a small number of accounts by women involved in European resistance movements or as survivors of the Nazi concentration camps. The most notable of these were *The Diary of Anne Frank*, Micheline Maurel's *Ravensbruck* and Anne-Marie Walters's *Moondrop to Gascony*. It was only in the 1980s that women's records of their wartime experiences began to be published, often from letters, diaries, and manuscripts which had lain ignored for many decades.[3]

As Dorothy Sheridan, one of those active in the recovery of these writings, has observed:

Fantasies of adventure, courage and militarism associated with warfare have usually been seen as a male preserve. Women were not expected to share in this sense of adventure. Since the emergence of a new wave of feminism in the seventies and eighties, however, there has been renewed interest in the more active role played by women in the Second World War. A current debate focuses on the degree to which the economic demands of war, by forcing small changes, enabled women to break out of strictly gender-defined roles. The enthusiasm for reclaiming women's lost or "hidden" history has led us to look to the war period for images with which to identify. We can be Rosie the Riveter with our spanner, turban and dungarees. We can be in the Resistance, cycling round France in our summer frocks with our clandestine wireless sets strapped inside our rucksacks.[4]

This chapter discusses a number of the most well known "war" books published in the 1950s, which between them sold in millions and were read in even larger numbers. They formed the staple reading diet of myself and most of my school peers, and the sales figures suggest that they constituted the main reading of much of the adult British reading public too. The following list gives the titles, publication dates and number of editions of some of the most well known:

Moondrop to Gascony, Anne-Marie Walters, 1946 (paperback edition 1951)

The Wooden Horse, Eric Williams, 1949 (9 editions by 1965)

The Dam Busters, Paul Brickhill, 1951 (21 editions by 1968)

The Great Escape, Paul Brickhill, 1951

The Bridge over the River Kwai, Pierre Boulle, 1952 (17 editions by 1968)

The Colditz Story, P.R. Reid, 1952 (14 editions by 1974)

The White Rabbit, Bruce Marshall, 1952 (4 editions by 1954)

Two Eggs on My Plate, Oluf Reef Olsen, 1952 (3 editions by 1955)

The Naked Island, Russell Braddon, 1952

Boldness Be My Friend, Richard Pape, 1953 (6 editions by 1972)

The Diary of Anne Frank, 1953, (45 editions by 1981)

Scourge of the Swastika, Lord Russell of Liverpool, 1954 (16 editions by 1976)

Bomber Pilot, Leonard Cheshire, 1954 (298,000 copies sold, undated)

House of Dolls, Ka-Tzetnik 185683, 1956 (10 editions by 1958)

Camp on Blood Island, J.M. White & V. Guest, 1958 (6 editions in 1958)

Cockshell Heroes, C.E. Lucas Phillips, 1956

Knights of the Bushido, Lord Russell of Liverpool

Ill Met By Moonlight, W. Stanley Moss, 1956

Ravensbruck, Micheline Maurel, 1959

(This list is by no means definitive, and details as to publishing history are those contained in the copies collected over the years. Some of these books have continued to be reprinted, and only paperback titles are listed.)

There were many other books written about the war which were not always taken up by paperback publishers, or promoted as potential best-sellers in the genre. Some of these books evinced a politics distinct from what was generally published and promoted, and included what were probably two of the finest novels about the experiences of combatants of the Second World War: Alexander Baron's *From the City, From the Plough* (1948) and Dan Billany's *The Trap* (1950), both written by working-class socialists. Their view was frequently at odds with the way in which a popular cultural history of the war was being reconstructed in popular literature during the era of the Cold War. When I interviewed Baron in 1983, he said that,

> After the war, the first novels to get published were all by officers. Either by officers or people who'd come through *Penguin New Writing*, which was a great influence at the time. Stories were by the kind of intellectuals to whom the army was an agony. They wrote about it as an awful experience, sleeping with thirty-five ruffians. The officers didn't seem to have the Robert Graves touch, or that of Graves and Sassoon, who knew the Tommies were the men getting the rough end of the stick.[5]

Stuart Hood's *Pebbles From My Skull* (1963), which was contrarian in both its sensibility and politics, was published at a much later date than the majority of wartime accounts and thus entered "literature" in a different guise and through a different door. Too late to intervene and disturb the consensus of popular war literature in the 1950s, it nevertheless helped inspire a wave of popular autobiographical writing in Britain during the 1970s. The final paragraph became one of the most widely quoted epigrams of that time:

> We may record the past for various reasons: because we find it interesting; because by setting it down we can deal with it more easily; because we wish to escape from the prison where we face our individual problems, wrestle with our particular temptations, triumph in solitude and in solitude accept defeat and death. Autobiography is an attempted jail-break. The reader tunnels through the same dark.[6]

What does and does not get published and promoted was crucial to the framing and construction of popular memory and popular consciousness. The mainstream literature of the Second World War can be reasonable divided into four distinct genres: escape stories, heroism in war, stories of resistance, and testimonies of German and Japanese war crimes. Each genre had its distinctive traits and conventions; each genre has over time developed successors in popular literature and new forms of development, a not unsurprising occurrence since popular literature, like all other forms of popular culture, is a historical phenomenon and proceeds by adaptation and development. Thus escape stories flowed back into the consistently popular genre of prison literature; the tales of heroism developed into the male adventure novels of such writers as Alistair MacLean and Jack Higgins; the resistance novels formed part of the literary culture of post-war existentialism; and the literature of the war crimes was superseded by the Nazi war novels of such writers as Sven Hassel, H.H. Kirst and the fictional Nazi nightmares described by John Sutherland in his chapter on war literature in *Bestsellers: Popular Fiction of the 1970s*.[7]

Escape Stories

Escape stories of the First and Second World Wars are exceptional within the wider genre of prison literature in that they deal, unusually, with the experiences of the middle and upper classes under prison conditions. There was not one account of a prison escape by a rank and file member of the Services published as far as I can tell, though clearly such men made escape attempts and no doubt some succeeded. The first "escape" book, and probably the best, was Eric Williams's *The Wooden Horse*, first published in 1949. The story is well known: Williams and two other officers dug a tunnel out of the prison camp, by digging each day from under a wooden vaulting horse placed near the fence, used for exercise by other prisoners who were party to the plan. The escape was successful and, using forged passes, Williams and one other managed to travel to a seaport on the Baltic and get to Denmark. They later travelled on to England, with the help of members of the Danish resistance and French Communist workers billeted in Germany.

Williams' account of the routines of prison life remains the most detailed and convincing of all these books. He spent time portraying other prisoners and the effect of imprisonment on them, even acknowledging without irony the occasionally beneficial effects on himself and his fellow prisoners of such virtues as domestication and mutual support. His portrayal of a hut-mate, David, who retreated into a fantasy world of running a farm in his own imagination, is both moving and convincing writing. Other writers in the genre never even saw imprisonment as a particular social condition, with a history and a psychology, and describe prison life as little different from dormitory life at public school. Much the most frightening part of *The Wooden Horse* deals with the journey through Germany to the Baltic, along with days of waiting to make contact with a boat that would smuggle them onwards. During this time they had to pretend to be foreign workers with authorised travel permits and risked being caught, and possibly shot, every hour of the day. Williams is honest enough to admit that for much of the time when they were on the run he would rather have been back in the prison camp, so great was the fear and nightmare of discovery. After the war Williams went on to become a writer and the biographical note that prefaces the paperback edition of *The Wooden Horse* shows exactly how these escape accounts were framed in a context of rugged individualism and led on to the popular literature of male adventure:

> He now travels the world, by Land Rover and a small boat, and writes adventure novels which continue the theme of his escape books — man alone, struggling to preserve his freedom and integrity in spite of the odds against him.

P.R. Reid's *Colditz Story*, first published in 1952, was also filmed and made into a popular television series in the 1970s. Even more than Williams's publisher, Reid introduces his account in terms of war and imprisonment as a backcloth for the more important values of individualism and masculinity:

> The inspiration of escape books lives in men's memories and serves to keep alive the spirit of adventure. I can think of no other sport that is the peer of escape, where freedom, life, and loved ones are the prize of victory, and death the possible though by no means inevitable price of failure.

There is something ironic about this notion of freedom, which for the officer class producing these memoirs was associated with the escape from the collective living patterns of the prison camps. By contrast, in popular representations of working-class mores during the war, it is that sense of enforced collectivity and communal identity which is celebrated as being one of the most important values that emerged. Here are two definitions of freedom which appear to be in complete opposition: in one it is a quality associated with splendid isolation, in another it is associated with the commonality of things and the mutual aid of interlocking relationships. The civic values of such exhortatory films as Humphrey Jennings's *London Can Take It*, emphasising the collective resistance spirit of working-class London during the Blitz, living together in bomb shelters and all pulling together, is at the opposite end of the pole to the private values exemplified in these accounts of escape and heroic individualism.

Colditz Story is permeated by public-school, officer class values; not surprising in that Colditz was for "none but officers", particularly those who had already made escape attempts from other camps which Reid ironically described as "prep-schools". As officers they received relatively fair treatment, and were not expected to work, unlike the majority of prisoners of the Germans incarcerated in labour camps where, as is known, they died or were murdered in their millions once their labour power had been exhausted. In Colditz the prisoners ordered a grand piano for their theatre — and got it. They frequently refused orders *en masse* and escaped punishment.

Paul Brickhill's *The Great Escape* is a more sombre story, for what started out as another escape story from a fairly benevolently run prison camp ends suddenly with the arbitrary execution of the majority of the escapees as a result of the direct orders of Hitler, an act that horrified people in Britain at the time and clearly haunted Brickhill himself. The majority of Brickhill's close colleagues were RAF Officers and public-school educated. The tunnel that was the means of "the great escape" took nearly a year to dig, and while that was going on some fifty men worked on forging documents, three to five hours a day for the same period. Some eighty prisoners managed to escape and fifty were shot when captured, wherever they were caught.

The RAF officer, shot down over Europe, captured, imprisoned and then escaping, became an early archetypal hero of post-war popular literature. During the first years of the war airmen were the ones most likely to be captured and imprisoned, since during that period engagements between Britain and Germany took the form of "the war in the air". In the second half of the war, particularly in North Africa and the Far East, the majority of British men taken prisoner were from the ranks of the army. In the Second World War, however, the RAF acquired a reputation as the heroic elite of the three services, and the aviator, or airman quickly attained an almost mythical status in public consciousness, though this iconic status had already been prepared.

In Britain and across Europe the airman had already become a commanding figure and symbol in the poetry and prose of the 1920s and 1930s. Yeats' great poem *An Irish Airman Foresees His Death* had been published in 1919:

A lonely impulse of delight
Drove to this tumult in the clouds;
I balanced all, brought all to mind,
The years to come seemed waste of breath,
A waste of breath the years behind
In balance with this life, this death.

The helmeted figure of the airman also appears in a number of Auden's poems in the 1930s. The lyrical novels of the French aviator and writer Saint-Exupery were being translated and published during this period too. One of the most disturbing novels published near the beginning of the war was Rex Warner's *The Aerodrome* (1941), which described the takeover of a village by an authoritarian air force based nearby, dedicated to fascistic concepts of efficiency, order and moral discipline. And the poetry that captured most people's imaginations during the war was John Pudney's aircrew poetry, notably *For Johnny* from his collection *Dispersal Point and Other Air Poems* (1942).

Yet though it is understandable that great heroism was attached to the fighter pilots who were defending British cities against enemy bombing, it seems strange in retrospect that while such heroism was attributed to the crews of high-altitude bombers, much less attention was given to the equally selfless courage of the women and men, for example, who either directly risked their lives in the maintenance of defence and civilian services, or served as foot soldiers and tank crews in the Western Desert, or as sailors on the North Atlantic convoys.

One of the appeals of the escape books lay in the minutiae of disguise, counterfeit and subterfuge which the escapers employed to get them out of the prison camps and back to their own country. Part of the fascination of prison literature is concerned with how people manage patiently and with great ingenuity to turn tiny resources into major systems of routine survival.[8] The childish fascination with disguise, magical deception and illusionism, is fully addressed in the details of these books. The ingenuity was astonishing. Eric Williams's companion, described in *The Wooden Horse*, was able to counterfeit work-permits in a couple of hours, reproducing by hand German gothic type, impregnating papers and cardboards with colours rinsed from curtain material, all achieved in a hotel room the night before they had to be used. In Colditz a Polish prisoner constructed a typewriter out of wood, which could be dis-assembled in seconds, and was used to type out forged documents for would-be escapers.

Paul Brickhill has a whole chapter on the work of "The Forgers" in *The Great Escape*, describing how prisoners worked in production units able to turn out imitation German uniforms, replica guns, workmen's clothes of different nationalities, compasses, headed notepaper and other accessories for the escapers. They also built a duplicator that used the gelatine extracted from invalid jellies and an ink made out of the lead from pencils. Similarly the tunnels they dug were masterpieces of resourcefulness and deception. The interest of all this detail, the iconography of deception and disguise, is, of course, not simply due to a nostalgia for wartime conditions and necessity. The appeal lies in that sense which every reader has that people can change their identity, change their name, disappear and start a different life somewhere else. Illusionism and masquerade are traditional features of popular theatre and literary forms. The escape literature of the Second World War appealed to that already existing aspect of popular sensibility. In mainland Britain many civilians actually used the social disruption of war to migrate and start new lives.

Heroism in War

By far the largest group of books about the war were those detailing extraordinary fighting missions, or the activities of secret agents where particular kinds of courage or daring were required. As such they, too, took on the forms and narrative styles of the popular genres of adventure stories or tales of dangerous exploration. The largest number of them dealt with the accounts of fighter pilots or leaders of audacious bombing expeditions, including Paul Brickhill's *Reach for the Sky* and *The Dam Busters*, Guy Gibson's *Enemy Coast Ahead*, Richard Hillary's *The Last Enemy* and Richard Pape's *Boldness Be My Friend*. These books, together with the RAF prison-escape literature, more than any other war books, provided two of the most important images of the Britain that had gone to war in 1939, and hence the Britain that had to be preserved after the war was over. The first was the evocation of a rural England of country houses, village pubs, public schools, Oxbridge and expensive sports cars. The second was the representation of Britain at war as a second Elizabethan era.

The portrait of England that Eric Williams conjured up was "the sunshine on the Cambridge countryside and the whiteness of the clouds above", or, "driving the Aston Martin fast down the Great North Road in the early morning with the open road long and straight and empty in front of you..." His fellow escapee recalls "Oxford and a houseboat on the Thames... His brother home from

Sandhurst; and drinking pints. Janet poling a punt under the green shade of the willows, the water dropping from the pole in a cascade of diamonds and himself lying in a punt and watching her." H.E. Bates in his introduction to *Escape or Die* described the world the pilots left behind them as one of "cool beers and English lawns", or breathing the "calm summer air of an English village". Guy Gibson evoked a "peaceful England on a cool spring evening; the flowers are blooming, the hum of serenity is in the air." Leslie Bell's Lt. Col. Elder Ellis, a senior officer responsible for supplying resistance organisations with weapons, is portrayed at home at the end of the war: "But if he looks across from his garden he can see silhouetted against the skyline, Windsor Castle itself. It stands there untouched by enemy hands; solid, durable, strangely symbolic of what we have and are...."

To quote these images is in no way to denigrate the courage and achievements of these pilots and their crews; this was the England they had been schooled in and wished to preserve. But it was not everybody's England, or Britain, and hardly any other images or evocations of that other Britain appeared in the books that were usually considered as constituting the key books about the war. None of the writers registered that there were many versions of Britain, of which theirs was only one. There were too few accounts by servicemen and women in the ranks who had grown up in a Britain where mass unemployment, urban slums, rural poverty, relieving officers, tied cottages and other manifestations of a society divided by class or inheritance, still formed part of daily life.

If anything, the reverse was the case. The war allowed the creation of new national mythologies. It was the short-story writer and novelist, H.E. Bates, who in his introduction to the escape stories collected in *Escape or Die* wrote:

It has been said, and I think with a great deal of truth, that the RAF were the new Elizabethans, fighting and adventuring in the air, as the great navigators had fought and adventured in the seas.[9]

Bates's most popular novel, *Fair Stood the Wind for France* (1944), was an account of a British bomber crew forced down over France. The title comes from the Elizabethan poem by Michael Drayton "The Battle of Agincourt". The same year witnessed the showing of Laurence Olivier's *Henry V,* consciously made to revive memories of earlier English battles in France and was unapologetically part of the battle of ideas and ideals. The film score was by William Walton.

Shakespeare was invoked on many other occasions, not least by the titles that writers chose for their war testimonies. Airey Neave's account of his escape from Colditz was called *They Have Their Exits* (*As You Like It*, Act II, vii, line 141); Richard Pape's story of capture, imprisonment and torture became *Boldness be My Friend*, (*Cymbeline* Act I, vi, line 18); W. Stanley Moss called his account of the abduction of a key German general from his headquarters in Crete in 1944 *Ill Met by Moonlight* (*Midsummer Night's Dream*, Act II, i, line 60).

While much of the literature of the First World War simply wished to reinstate that long Edwardian era which had just been disrupted by the war, there had been no long reach back into the past on that occasion. During the Second World War, however, the England evoked by the mythology of Agincourt and the rural arcadia of *A Midsummer Night's Dream* was one of robust yeomanry, rustic sensuality and courtly love, as well as the occasional dangerous assignation under the cover of night.

Stories of the Resistance

In his study of European resistance movements during the Second World War M.R.D. Foot wrote, "Resisters tend to be out of step with their time usually in advance of it..."[10] It was true that in the resistance movement, many conventional social relations had to be subverted or circumvented. Thus women played a key role; and in the literature we are dealing with this is the one category where two of the most popular books dealt with the heroic exploits of women: Jerrard Tickell's *Odette: Story of a British Agent* and Anne-Marie Walters's *Moondrop to Gascony*. But other social relations were subverted by the contingencies and exigencies of war. Those whose work conventionally commanded a low social status — such as railway workers, shop workers, typists, clerks, garage mechanics — were found to be working in jobs that were strategic and essential to the continuance of everyday life. Because they were, to some extent, socially invisible, this meant they were less likely to be suspected of playing important roles in resistance movements, which many of them did.

In resistance stories it was impossible not to mention the role of communists and socialist militants in these life and death struggles, and this was probably the first time that such militants appeared in a favourable light in popular English writing. One also learned through these accounts and testimonies which classes and sections of the society embraced collaboration and which didn't. The literature of resistance was unavoidably political and, unusually in popular literature, had frequently to align the forces of good (exemplified by patriotism, honour, courage) with people not normally considered as possessing these qualities: communist workers, trade unionists, itinerants and marginal groups such as sailors, prostitutes and criminals, as well as bourgeois nationalists and social-democratic politicians.

It was for precisely such reasons of social dislocation that conventional strategists of war such as Sir Basil Liddell Hart worried about the political implications of recognising the importance of civilian resistance because the "social dangers inherent in it, for the future of a settled society."[11] One of the Dutch resistance slogans encompassed this understanding that conventional social relations could never be the same again: "Only dead fishes float down the stream, live ones swim against it."[12]

Some resistance stories were presented as genre writing. This is true of such books as MacGregor Urquhart's *Partisan*, the story of an escaped British POW who joined the Italian resistance. The cover blurb claims that: "This is a nerve-tearing tale of hard combat in Tunisia and imprisonment in Italy, followed by a wildly exciting life on the run in company with the Italian partisans. It is crammed with hard dramatic action and spine-chilling crises so cannot fail to enthral even the most shock-hardened reader."

Similarly, a book such as Gunby Hadath's *Men of the Maquis* (1947) is told as a series of audacious adventure stories in which the enemy appear to be just other individuals, *"les Boches"* rather than fascists. The word "fascism" rarely appears in the many books that make up that extensive literature of the war, and the impression thus gained was that it was essentially a war of competing national interests rather than of irreconcilable ideologies. Whether this was because keen editors were apt to pencil out any passages of attempted political analysis by the narrators — in case it bogged down the fast flow of the narrative — or because the writers had self-censored themselves in advance in deference to narrow notions about the ingredients of successful stories we do not know.

Anne-Marie Walters' *Moondrop to Gascony* is quite different. Although her story is told from the point of view of a British subject, she was of English-French parentage. Walters' account of her work as a British secret agent in France is as much a reflection on her own sense of what her life was being lived for as it is a narrative of clandestine espionage activities. The story contains a number of reflections on her own mental states, her sense of having no other choices in a war in which fascism for a long time appeared to be able to win, as well honestly exploring her fears of death: these qualities make it all the more moving, and even exceptional.

Few French and Italian accounts of resistance were translated and published in Britain. What were translated after the war were those fictional accounts such as Jean-Paul Sartre's trilogy *The Roads to Freedom*, Simone de Beauvoir's *The Blood of Others* and Camus's allegory *The Plague*. These developed the experience of the resistance into the post-war political and cultural aesthetic of existentialism, influential as a cultural mood in many European countries, and extending far beyond that of being a mere coterie fashion. Certainly Sartre, de Beauvoir and Camus were widely read in Britain, much more than many British novelists writing at the time. This was largely because few if any British writers were in a position to explore that distinctive political/literary aesthetic which grew out of that major historical nightmare, the fascist occupation of central Europe. Sadly, too soon, this was augmented by a new — if less deadly — form of occupation in eastern Europe, that of Soviet communism.

The Literature of the Holocaust
"After the Holocaust," Theodor Adorno famously wrote, "lyric poetry is impossible." Yet there had to be writing, otherwise only a few people would ever know exactly what happened in the concentration camps in Europe and the prisoner-of-war camps run by the Japanese in Malaya and Burma. Of all the genres of war literature it is the literature of the concentration camps which continues to exercise a compulsive fascination and morbidity. Such books as *Scourge of the Swastika*, *The Naked Island* continue to be reprinted, even though it has always been apparent that on many occasions such books have been read — and even promoted through the imagery of the book-covers — as part of the pornography of sadism.

One of the first accounts published in Britain by a survivor of the Buchenwald camp was *The Dungeon Democracy* (1945) by Christopher Burney. It remains a mystery why this was never published in paperback or promoted as so many others were, since it is a very rare account by a British soldier of the experience of one of the concentration camps. But Burney himself predicted a later flood of books after his own, full of "words of self-righteousness", whereas Burney's account is not so much anti-German or anti-Nazi, as rather completely pessimistic about humanity *per se*. For the book has a theme — which is that the prisoners at Buchenwald could have organised themselves into a united body of resistance, but they failed to do so. In Burney's account the prisoners stuck together in groups on the basis of nationality and simply fended for themselves. This question of why there was so little resistance in the camps was raised later on and became quite contentious (and also a little anti-Semitic once again), for it revived that commonplace political tactic of blaming the victims. Burney's account actually doesn't do this; for him the terrifying thing about Buchenwald was that it revealed how superficial notions of individual morality actually were, and how rapidly people would accede to the exigencies of other environments.

Burney's next book, *Solitary Confinement* (1952), an account of his capture in France as a British agent and his year in solitary confinement before being sent to Buchenwald, did get published in paperback and went through a number of editions. This followed the traditional genre of prison literature, being mostly a series of reflections on loneliness, isolation and human self-sufficiency. Russell Braddon's, *The Naked Island*, first published in 1952 and still in print, is the best-known account of life as a Japanese prisoner-of-war. While the Japanese did not have a programme of mass murder of prisoners as did the Nazi regime, many thousands of prisoners died as a result of exhaustion through forced labour and the lack of any kind of care through adequate diet or living conditions. Braddon does raise one of the few questions in these books that refers to class inequalities back in Britain, which otherwise appears as the embodiment of everything that is best and perfect in a nation. He reports that the British prisoners died much more easily of dysentery than the fitter, healthier Australians who had enjoyed a much better standard of living as civilians before the war.

The health of many of the British soldiers was poor when they had joined up as a result of poverty in the Britain of the 1930s. But Braddon's account is fuelled by a terrible racism which, though understandable at the time when it was first written, remains uncorrected or unmodified in subsequent editions. For him, the war "of Asia against the white man" will go on forever and is in Braddon's terms endemic. One can only assume that he had not then read any accounts of the Nazi atrocities performed in the name of an ideology which was that of "the white man" carried to extremes.

The most comprehensive account of the horrors of German fascism was *The Scourge of the Swastika: A Short History of Nazi War Crimes* by Lord Russell of Liverpool, first published in 1954 and more or less reprinted and reissued every year since then. It is described by its author in the preface as being,

> ...intended to provide the ordinary reader with a truthful and accurate account of many of these German war crimes. It has been compiled from the evidence given and the documents produced at various war-crime trials, and from statements made by eye-witnesses of war crimes to competent war-crime investigation commissions in the countries where they were committed.

I had always been prejudiced against this book, mostly because I believed it was read as a kind of pornography, and I suspected the intentions of the writer and its publishers. In fact, re-reading it today, I believe it is a sober and genuinely horrified account, nightmarish in its details, whose publication has been consistently justified.

More worrying was the treatment of women's accounts of the camps, such as Micheline Maurel's *Ravensbruck* (1958) and *House of Dolls* (1956) by Ka-Tzetnik 135633, which were published in ways that framed them as part of the pornography of sadism. Micheline Maurel's book, sincerely and despairingly written, has on its cover a full-breasted woman in a skimpy dress with pouting red lips pressed against a barbed wire fence. *The House of Dolls* emphasises that it is a story of enforced prostitution and on the front cover has the words, "It shows the depths of bestiality to which Germans sank under Hitler..." In both cases the publishing format itself contributes to the ambiguity of motive with which such books could be read. These "framing" devices, so characteristic of paperback design in the mass market, were typical of so much publishing in that time, and in retrospect appear highly dubious.

Yet the book that remains the most poignant of all has also been the most popular. *The Diary of Anne Frank*, first published in Britain in 1953 and since then endlessly reprinted, suggesting that once again people find it difficult to encompass tragedy and barbarism on a huge scale and have to find its meaning through the plight of an individual, and through that most personal of forms, the diary. And, paradoxically, there is something about a diary entry, with its absolute specificity of time and place, that precisely locates the situation of the original author, thus creating a sense of "timelessness" which eludes most other writing seeking to achieve the same effect. Whenever a reader begins to read Anne Frank's diary, for the first or the twentieth time, there is always that young woman, secreted away, writing at a desk, with a still uncertain future lying ahead.

Thus all these narratives of war developed into specific genres for that period and after that slowly fed back into other mainstream genres of popular literature: prison literature, male heroism, resistance and politics, and a new one of Nazi revivalism. Two of these genres continued to dominate male reading for a long time after. For example, Alistair MacLean's first novel, *HMS Ulysses*, was set on a ship escorting a Russian convoy through the North Sea and into the Arctic Circle during the war. Since then all MacLean's novels, almost all set in exclusively male settings — a nuclear submarine, an oil rig, a commando squad — have been popular bestsellers. Seventeen of MacLean's books have sold over one million copies each, and have made him, according to John Sutherland, "the best-selling English novelist ever".[13] More disturbing have been the novels of writers such as H.H. Kirst, Sven Hassell, and Leon Kessler, all of whom produce violent war books based on the exploits of German commando units with such titles as *Cauldron of Blood*, *Slaughter Ground*, *Otto's Blitzkrieg*, which not only breach the boundaries of traditional genre, but also of morality and good taste.

Three Dissenting Writers

There were however some books which recorded the daily misery and horrors of the war from the point of view of ordinary combatants: the "poor bloody infantry". Alexander Baron's *From the City, From the Plough* (1948) has already been mentioned. Many reviewers at the time considered it the best novel written about the war by a British writer. V.S. Pritchett, doyen of literary reviewers, thought it "the only war book that has conveyed any sense of reality to me", while *The Daily Worker* described it as "the finest book to appear in Britain concerning the Second World War", an opinion echoed in several of Baron's obituaries.[14] Baron, East London born, Jewish, Labour League of Youth organiser and, in 1946, demobbed soldier, wrote this heartfelt novel at nights, feeling a need to redress the balance away from the officers' point of view, as was observed at the beginning of this chapter.

From the City, From the Plough is set in an army camp on the South Downs as one battalion waits for the invasion of Normandy to begin. They will be landed in France to start the final offensive against the Germans. All of Baron's characters are working-class men, fully developed as individuals with inner lives of their own, and he allows them to talk about their civilian lives and the conditions of life and work they have come from before the army. Here is a portrait of a Britain that simply isn't there in most of the other books: the struggle for survival in the slums of the big cities, casual labour, poor health and little hope for the future. There are also those who have come from the rural areas where, as labourers, they and their parents before them have been worked to exhaustion on the land in order to earn the means of survival only. In Baron's male community there are no heroics, no great manly virtues, but rather we are shown a group of men thrown together, learning to live with each other, many of them frightened, trying to make the best out of a situation which they no longer control. They comfort each other, sort out squabbles, try to learn to live communally — and wait.

The battle scenes that follow the final landing are horrendous, more shocking and convincing than those to be found in most other books of this kind. Only a handful of the characters we have met survive. The values that emanate from Baron's book are not those of some mythologised "England" or specious nationalism, but of a class that puts the welfare of others, mutual support and solidarity, above the values of individualism and self-interest. Whereas the heroes of so much popular war literature are always shown to be fighting in order to preserve the past, the soldiers in *From the City, From the Plough* are shown to be fighting for a different future.

After *From the City, From the Plough* Baron wrote three more books about the war: *There's No Home* (1950) deals with a brief interlude between the fighting for a group of British soldiers in Sicily; *With Hope, Farewell* (1952) is the story of a young Jewish pilot who is badly injured in a crash and who cannot settle down to civilian life after the war. A very fine collection of short stories, *The Human Kind* (1953), is built around small incidents in people's lives just before, during and just after the war. A lot of detail in these stories is concerned with the traumas of fighting and the social dislocation caused by the war, and the problem, particularly for men, of re-building a "post-war self". In these stories, for a change, there is no false sentimentality or Little Englandism. In one story, "Scum of the Earth", a drunken squaddie pours out a monologue of hate against all foreigners, the "wogs" and the "wops", to whom, "it's no use talking, it's only your fist they understand." He goes on to recount in great detail his rape and humiliation of the young Italian girl he found rifling the dustbins of the camp for food, and continues by inveighing against her degradation and sexual promiscuity. Jingoism, ignorance and sadism are all combined in a horrible portrait of British arrogance and self-righteousness. But there are also very moving stories of human decency and self-effacing generosity, particularly in the ranks.

The work of Dan Billany is even less known than that of Baron, yet his two accounts of the war are amongst the most moving of any published. Little is known about Billany other than that he died after escaping from an Italian prisoner-of-war camp in 1944.[15] The manuscripts of the two books written while he was a prisoner were given to an Italian farmer (presumably by Billany himself) who after the war sent them on to Billany's parents, who in turn sent them to a publisher.

Billany attended an elementary school in Hull which he left in 1928. His first job was as an errand boy. Three years later he attended classes for unemployed young people and went on to pass sufficient examinations to be able to go to Hull University from 1934 to 1937. He became an English teacher and on the outbreak of war joined "C" Company of the 4th Battalion, East Yorkshire Regiment which was posted to North Africa in 1942 and which, on 1 June that year, came under severe attack from Rommel's Eighth Army with many British soldiers being taken prisoner, including Billany. They were taken to Italy where they were put into prison camps. It was in his prison camp that Billany wrote *The Trap* and, with the collaboration of another prisoner, David Dowie, *The Cage*. The order in which they were written remains unknown, but *The Cage* was published first, in 1949, when, as it says on the book cover, "the fates of the two authors" were still unknown.

In the introduction to *The Cage* Billany and Dowie argued for the importance of writing directly about their situation: "If we delayed writing till we got back to England we should gain in tranquillity, but in everything else we should lose." The style of the book is unusual in that it is made up of short episodes, discussions on paper between the two writers, portraits of other prisoners, and, in the final section, the story of an infatuation between two men, a love for each other that is denied by both any form of physical expression. Unlike most other portraits of prison camp life, *The Cage* consciously lacks heroics, concentrating on the disturbing shifts and pressures of prison camp life (including the breakdown of traditional masculine values). It ignores the possibility of escape in preference to reflections on the question of the larger prison beyond the camp walls. The authors even suggest that their prison experience has freed them from some things:

> Soon now we shall go out from here — back into the world. How many of us will be truly freed — none, I suppose. But some must have gained a certain freedom from prison; the prison of walls and wire must have helped them out of the prison of mistrust.

Billany's hand is often recognisable by its political acuity and fondness for striking metaphors and aphorisms that give the singly written novel, *The Trap*, its greater strength and aesthetic integrity. In one of the entries in *The Cage*, Billany describes the relationship between fascism and the architecture of the local orphanage where they are being kept temporarily, a building erected in the era of Mussolini's state programme:

> Exit the sham-eternal, Fontanello Orphanage, type of Fascism. Hundreds of tons of extraneous masonry piled

along the facade, but the whole building shakes when a few people jump on an upstairs floor... it looks like the Parthenon, but it will vanish in the night. And even so it will outlast the fascism that built it, and children whose parents have been killed by fascism will trace their shadowed lives back to this cheap building. Pretension. The attempt to freeze the flow of life, to impose a pattern on events. Reality laughs at such attempts. You can't cage the future, it will have its way. To build a rigid social system which would last forever, what a hope. The only thing that never changes is Change.

The Trap is Billany's most important book (he had published two short novels before the war). It is a tragic novel about the break-up of relatively settled, though harsh, patterns of working-class life by the advent of war, and the prospect of permanent cultural fragmentation. The first two-thirds of the novel concern the love affair between the narrator, a young middle-class officer, and a working-class woman, Elizabeth. They marry before he leaves for Africa, and the last third of the novel concerns his experience of the desert war and his capture by the Germans and Italians. The novel ends with the narrator's arrival in an Italian prison camp.

The context of much of the first part of the novel is the family life of Elizabeth, and it is Billany's attempt to portray the material difficulties of working-class life in the 1930s in Britain. The characters are well realised, the story flows, with intervening moments of personal and social tragedy as the war bites into the lives of the families in the town where the narrator is stationed. Yet what gives *The Trap* its lasting status as a highly original and political novel is the reflectiveness and aphoristic quality of the writing. When the narrator interrupts the narrative to address the reader, as Billany does often in *The Trap*, one is reminded very much of a sensibility strangely similar to Walter Benjamin's. Two such aphorisms about history that are found in *The Trap* might well have come from Benjamin:

But our eyes. They will reveal our blight to the future —
Unfilled Hope. Eternal Hope. Unrealised Hope. We only
live in Hope: in hope that tomorrow will give us that
unknown satisfaction which, yesterday, Hope expected
today... The Present is a room; the Past furnishes it, the
Future lights it.

Much of the third chapter of the novel is made up of a
lengthy disquisition on the way in which the working-class
has been portrayed historically in the novel:

It used to be the fashion to see the working-class always
from a little distance — if not through bars, at least
through an impervious psychological screen, so that their
actions and emotions were as irrelevant to the gentle
Writer and the gentle Reader as those of flatfish on the
floor of their aquarium, on the other side of their thick
glass and in their own bottle-green element.
As examples of Humble Worth, the working-class at one
time challenged the dog... (As a literary device)

One can understand how such insights set Billany's work
against the conventions of popular war literature, in
which "the other ranks" still functioned as a foil to the
individual achievements of their officers.

The achievement of *The Trap* is that it manages to combine many usually separate genres and modes of writing
while remaining an integrated whole. It is a moving and by
no means sentimental love story; it is also a novel of
working-class family life shattered by war; it is a war
novel, too, and a genuinely frightening one; but it is also a
novel about writing a novel, about how to write a novel
(under prison conditions) that is a political polemic and an
intervention into questions of literary aesthetics. And
towards the end biting questions about imperialist ideologies and their rationalisations are asked (ideologies that
unconsciously informed many other books about the cam-
paign in North Africa and the Far East). Writing of some
Egyptian peasants, the narrator asks the reader to see
that,

...those that destroyed them, mocked them. They that wasted them, demanded of them a song. To their foul injury they added foul insult — trod them into the dung, then called them "dirty wogs": starved them till their ribs showed white, and so that their children's shins were no thicker than a stick of celery — so that they prayed for even a crust — then "all wogs are beggars": kicked them till they flinched at a shadow — "shifty wogs": robbed them till there was nothing but their breath to steal, then "every wog is a thief..."[16]

If not the finest novel to come out of the war, it was the most experimental and intriguing. It was published by Faber in 1950 and reissued by the Readers' Union in 1952. It has had a sporadic publishing history since, reflecting the way in which the war has been reconstructed in popular literature since 1945, in which seminal books such as Billany's have been marginalised if not silenced.

The last of our books to have substantially rejected the mythology of war is Stuart Hood's *Pebbles From My Skull* (1963). This was clearly written as a result of a return visit by Hood to the region of Italy where he had been an escaped prisoner some twenty years earlier. It is both a reconstruction of that period and an inquiry into his own understanding of that experience. For again, here there is no heroic, selfless if dangerous flight back to England, but instead a developing interest in the country in which he found himself now "free" even though on the run. Hood spent from 8 September 1943 until 15 August 1944, nearly one whole year, at large in the hills and valleys of Chianti, sometimes fighting with the partisans, often on his own, "taking time out of life".

There are many similarities with Billany's experience. Hood found life outside prison — at least for the Italian peasants he met — actually harder than inside. In the countryside existence was "tied to a cycle of labour, and life mean, squalid, hard", an existence where some even looked forward to death as a release. In such accounts there are no abstract notions of "freedom" as some metaphysical quality that exists over and above the actual material reality of day-to-day life — there is just a variety of circumstances in which people struggle to create various kinds of freedoms.

Among the peasants in what became German-occupied Italy, Hood found the women braver than the men, but also found that effective resistance, or guerrilla struggles, were often as cruel in their methods and choices as those of the enemy they fought. And in saying this Hood, in the only reference in the book to the period in which it was written, suggests that readers might bear this in mind when thinking about the "terrorist" struggles that were then being waged in Cyprus against the British forces. The book concludes with a moving series of passages about what Hood learned from his "time out of life", of his understanding of what was still then an unchanging pattern of peasant life, culture and death, and the many examples of human solidarity that strangers showed him.

Baron, Billany and Hood created a literature out of the experience of the Second World War that went against the grain of accepted literary conventions. They are the only writers with whom one can compare the far more angular and tough-minded realism of the best of the American novels of this time, including Norman Mailer's *The Naked and the Dead*, James Jones's *From Here to Eternity* and Kurt Vonnegut's *Slaughterhouse 5*. The American writers at least acknowledged that what was being fought towards the end of the Second World War was no longer a war of soldiers and rifles but a technological war of saturation bombing, fire-bombing and the first use of atomic weapons — "total war", as we now understand it — though the theatre of war was sometimes different.

Most writing about the war published in Britain never came near an understanding of this. The great wave of books outlined above appeared some time after the war ended, in most cases in the early 1950s. The political climate was already changing away from the radical optimism of the 1945 "settlement". The return of a

Conservative Government in 1951, after a term of Labour rationing and austerity, meant that a war fought in the cause of anti-fascism and ending with a popular desire for radical change at home, was by then already in the process of being re-imagined and re-constructed as a war to preserve the old order, and in particular, a more pastoral definition of Englishness. The "Dambusters' March" began to be played at right-wing rallies, and evocations of the Dunkirk spirit were used to reinforce anti-European feeling, and the historian Lord Beloff countered the growing peace movement in Britain and Europe with the extraordinarily vicious assertion that, "What strengthens my conservatism is that for me a CND badge and a swastika are essentially interchangeable."

[1]Since this was written, there have been a number of new studies on the topic, including, Alan Munton, *English Fiction of the Second World War* (1989), Dorothy Sheridan, *Wartime Women: An Anthology of Women's Wartime Writing for Mass Observation* (1990), Adam Piette, *Imagination at War* (1995), Jenny Hartley's *Millions Like Us: British Women's Fiction of the Second World War* (1997), and Mark Rawlinson's *British Writing of the Second World War* (2000).

[2]Boris Ford, ed., *The Pelican Guide to English Literature: The Modern Age*, Harmondsworth, 1961; Robert Hewison, *Under Seige: Literary Life in London 1939-45*, London, 1979; Walter Allen, *Tradition and Dream*, Harmondsworth, 1965; Ronald Blythe, *Components of the Scene*, Harmondsworth, 1966.

[3]Such works of recovery include, *Nella Last's Diary 1939-45* (1981), Dorothy Sheridan, *Wartime Women: An Anthology of Women's Wartime Writing for Mass Observation* (1990).

[4]Dorothy Sheridan (1990), *op. cit.*, p.7.

[5]Interview with Alexander Baron, 7 June, 1983.

[6]Stuart Hood, *Pebbles From My Skull*, London, 1963, p.153.

[7]Even today, sixty years after the end of the war, a swastika on a book-cover remains a powerful selling icon.

[8]After the war, the survival strategies of those incarcerated in institutions became the subject of fascinating work by sociologists such as Erving Goffman.

[9]H.E. Bates, introduction to, Paul Brickhill, *Escape or Die*, London, 1954, p.10.

[10]M.R.D. Foot, *Resistance*, London, 1975, p.13.

[11]M.R.D. Foot (1975), *op. cit.*, p.316.

[12]M.R.D. Foot (1975), *op. cit.*, p.320.

[13]John Sutherland, *Best-sellers; Popular Fiction of the 1970s*, London, 1981, p.96.

[14]In his obituary of Baron in *The Guardian*, 8 December, 1999, John Williams describes Baron as "the greatest British novelist of the last war."

[15]Much more is now known about Billany thanks to the assiduous efforts of two Hull teachers, whose fictional account of Billany's life based on local and family research was published as *Dan Billany: Hull's lost hero* (1999, by Valerie A. Reeves and Valerie Showan (Hull, 1999).

[16]Dan Billany, *The Trap*, London, 1950, p.23.

Expressionism and
Working-Class Fiction

In his essay, "The Storyteller", Walter Benjamin distinguishes between two generic traditions of story-telling, symbolised by two contrasting occupations: the peasant and the voyager. "If one wants to picture these two groups through their archaic representatives," he wrote, "one is embodied in the resident tiller of the soil, and the other in the trading seaman."[1] One told the stories of the village, its people and its history, while the other brought stories from lands where people lived different lives according to different customs. Both traditions complemented each other. Benjamin's distinction remains valuable in contemporary arguments about finding cultural forms and processes which enable the balancing of the local and particular with the national and international. This is one of the most pressing contemporary political and cultural problems and currently finds its most developed expression in the controversies surrounding the achievements — and also the limitations — of the recent and widespread growth of local people's history projects.[2] This distinction is also useful to employ when looking back at one of the most energetic periods of working-class writing, the 1930s, because by doing so it becomes clear that most recent attention to the writing of that decade has been focused on just one of the traditions — the local — at the expense of understanding attempts to create a different aesthetic of working-class experience based not on place and continuity but on dislocation and transience.

For when we think of the working-class writers of the 1930s who made a permanent and popular impact, we think of the writers who took as their political and aesthetic ambition the project of describing the life of the communities they lived in, usually employing a literary technique most easily summarised as "documentary realism". The writers and books of that period whose names and titles are still recalled today would include for example, Walter Brierley with *Means Test Man*, B.L. Coombes with *These Poor Hands*, Willy Goldman with *East End My Cradle*, Walter Greenwood with *Love on the Dole*, Lewis Jones with *Cwmardy* and *We Live*, and John Sommerfield with *May Day*. (Lewis Grassic Gibbon's *A Scot's Quair* is, I personally feel, a quite singular and separate achievement in that decade.) All of these books were essentially literary documents rooted in the continuity of class and place. Not surprisingly they emanated from communities with strong local identities often occasioned by the predominance of a single local industry. Brierley was a Derbyshire miner; Coombes and Jones both worked in South Wales pits (though Coombes had experienced one dislocation of place in the move from Herefordshire to South Wales as a teenager in search of work); Greenwood wrote from the experience of life in industrial Salford; Goldman of life in the Jewish East End; and Sommerfield about the tightly-knit working-class districts of riverside London.

In such books the communities in which they are set are whole worlds in themselves and little reference is made to events, places and peoples beyond them. Continuity of employment, even in the same pit or factory as the father, is one kind of ambition either realised or thwarted by economic recession and large-scale unemployment. Continuity also of family life along the old patterns is also often represented as an ideal, sometimes achieved but often disrupted as liaisons go amiss and become the major sources of drama in the novels. The desire to affirm the significance of the everyday life in the pit villages and industrial towns of what was still "Unknown England" was encouraged by the developing oppositional aesthetics of that period.[3] The poetry of Auden, Spender, C. Day-Lewis and MacNeice explored the imagery of the derelict industrial North. Literary and journalistic figures like John Middleton Murray, John Lehmann and George Orwell were always keen to commission documentary reporting by workers of their conditions; and, of course, Mass Observation developed the particularity of place and time to the extent that the degree of detail became self-parodying. (In his report on *The Pub and The People*, one Mass Observer spent an evening in a Bolton pub counting how many times the spittoon was used each hour in relation to different customers smoking different cigarettes and drinking different drinks.) Family life, then, was portrayed as the natural cell of the working-class community, and the permanent continuity of place and employment were the buttresses needed to ensure that family life continued as it should.

A Different "Proletarian Fiction"

But such experience of class were by no means universal. For the many people brought up in single industry communities, with strong local traditions, there were as many for whom class was experienced as the dislocation of the generations, the rootlessness of city life, a succession of casual jobs and the constant search for employment — often involving moving from town to town. There was also often extreme psychological isolation. Such people, or at least the men among them, might have found some of their feeling and experiences represented in the work of three Liverpool-Irish writers of the 1920s and 1930s — George Garrett, James Hanley and Jim Phelan — who, with the exception of Hanley, have been largely forgotten. Yet for a time they were clearly developing a quite different tradition of working-class or "proletarian" literature, not unconnected with the fact that they were all completely displaced from settled working-class communities. Like Benjamin's other archaic representative of a different story-telling tradition, Garret, Hanley and Phelan were all seamen.

Phelan and Garrett certainly knew each other and met from time to time between voyages to have a drink and talk about books and writing. In his autobiography, *The Name's Phelan*, Jim Phelan recalled such meetings:

> One of the most enlivening experiences of those days was that I met Joe Jarrett (George Garrett) twice, in the intervals of his sea-going. He too had become a big, broad-shouldered fellow, was very certain of himself, and we behaved like two schoolboys when we met. To my surprise, he thought and spoke of himself as a writer, although nine-tenths of his time was spent in the stokeholds. Some of his stories were published, and one or two long poems — we drank the money down Bootle dock road.[4]

Hanley knew of them but never met them, but they could hardly have been unaware of his writings since his first novels published in the first half of the 1930s were all set among Liverpool-Irish dockside families or featured the same kind of men at sea. They were also all at different times contributing stories and articles to magazines like *The Adelphi*, *New Writing* and *Left Review*, and so would have been aware of each other's work.

Now while the links between these three men were so tenuous that one cannot properly regard them as having formed a conscious school of proletarian writing, neither should one try to understand their work only as the separate achievements of three different writers who happened to be at work in the same city during the same period. There are many similarities of theme, technical experimentation and acknowledgments of literary influences that make it possible to read their work together with greater insight than if read separately. Apart from the fact that all three had worked as seamen, they all shared a very deep interest in the expressionist drama of Ibsen, Strindberg and O'Neill which led them to explore nonrealist forms of fictionalising working-class life (which Hanley continued to do up until his death, sadly without the recognition his work deserved).

James Hanley

James Hanley was the first of these writers to be published.[5] His first novel, *Drift*, came out in 1930. He was born in 1901, one of twelve children, to an Irish family settled in Liverpool, and went to sea at the age of fourteen. He remained at sea for nine years, an avid reader by his own account all the while, and when he returned to life on shore permanently he settled with the idea of becoming a writer. *Drift* explored many of the themes to which he — and Garrett and Phelan — returned to time and time again. The novel tells the story of a young boy, Joe, who refuses to follow his father into work as a seaman on leaving school, and is shown to be less than enthusiastic about any kind of work at all. Already this represents a break from the pervasive notions of continuity of experience which characterise the major tendency of working-class novels in the 1930s. Joe is determined to find a different way of life to that of his parents, relations and neighbours, whom he regards as permanently trapped in a fixed cycle of exploited labour as well as being in the grip of a frightening religious tyranny. Joe experiences Liverpool not as a free and easy seaport town where material poverty was compensated for by communal solidarity, but as an expressionistic nightmare:

> And always ascending towards the heavens the clouds of smoke and grease and steam. The city was heaving up its guts. There it lay like some huge beast. Meanwhile Joe was tramping along in the direction of the river. The pavements were aflood with life. And the cold tang of dawn — one saw it in the pinched blue faces. On they swept. Swarming miraculous life. The human ambulance, a mighty phalanx sweeping down, down, down.

Joe is viewed with deep mistrust by the rest of his family for both spurning loyalty to the Catholic Church and for reading the "disgusting and atheistical" works of Zola and Joyce. Worse still he is carrying on an affair with a young prostitute. Sexuality, particularly adolescent sexuality, looms ominously in many of Hanley's novels. Sexuality is "an abyss of desire" which is likely to consume and devour. It stands in opposition to the declared values of proper family life and therefore can only be found away from the community in the twilight world of those who have rejected (or have been rejected by) the puritan certainties of those working-class communities where religion is a much more powerful ingredient of consciousness than are the material exigencies of class. Towards the end of the novel Joe is waiting in Lime Street hoping to catch sight of Jane, the prostitute he is infatuated with, and through his eyes the reader observes the relentless parade of misery and ugliness which is likely to finally overpower him: the bulls being driven down to the abattoir, the prostitutes with their intoxicated, blowsy charms, the drunks and vagrants, the ragged and hungry children, the hellfire soap box orators. Neither land nor sea offer anything of value or possibility to Joe as he thinks about his future life. Society is a deranged nightmare.

Socialist politics enter the novel only briefly, represented by the least convincing of any of the characters in *Drift*. The socialists are portrayed as middle and upper-class aesthetes who lounge about in each other's flats listening to Beethoven and talking about Tolstoy and modern sculpture. Such a portrait was clearly a deliberate misrepresentation by Hanley, for there certainly was a strong working-class socialist tradition in Liverpool in the 1920s and 1930s; Hanley obviously wanted to emphasise Joe's helpless position for which the expressionistic style was the most suitable. And expressionism is a way of portraying a process of crisis, not a way of formulating solutions. Joyce's Stephen Daedalus is very much a prototype for Hanley's Joe, but Hanley was remarkably successful in creating a convincing Liverpool dockland milieu for his character, and the twin daemonologies of religion and sexuality are portrayed with great power and authenticity. It must have been a shocking and disturbing book to have published in 1930. And for a first novel a major achievement.

Boy and *The Furys*

Even more shocking, however, was Hanley's next novel, *Boy*, published in 1931, which remains the work by which Hanley is best known. It went through three rapid reprints and was then banned for obscenity in 1934. It is dedicated to Nancy Cunard, the shipping heiress who became involved in the world of avant-garde art in the 1920s and, later, left-wing cultural politics in the 1930s. It was Nancy Cunard who organised the famous edition of *Left Review* in 1937 which was called "Authors Take Sides" and published the results of a widely distributed questionnaire on well-known writers' attitudes to the Spanish Civil War. The dedication also suggests something of the way in which relatively unknown working-class writers were able to get published in that period. It happened mostly by political patronage from left-wing intellectuals active in metropolitan literary life. Hanley was certainly encouraged and supported by both Cunard and John Lehmann; Garrett by John Middleton Murray, Lehmann and Orwell; Phelan principally by H.G. Wells.

Boy is a truly disturbing novel. It opens in the classroom of a slum school where a young boy is about to tell the headmaster that his parents have decided that he must leave school to go to work. The boy himself would like to stay on (like the main character in *Drift* he is positively terrified of having to join the treadmill of slum life and toil on which his parents have wasted their lives), but he is completely at the mercy of his tyrannical parents. The headmaster sees education as offering no hope to the working-class confronted by the demands of the economic system, "this huge machine that daily ground people's hopes beneath its wheels". Any resistance at home to his father's decision to get him a job at the docks is met by being beaten into senselessness while his mother looks on indifferently, her mind on the additional income which the boy's wages will bring into the house. Working-class male self-assertion and violence are portrayed by Hanley with great disgust and bitterness.

The novel, very simply written, gains a powerful allegorical weight by being quite unspecific about its geographical location. It is simply set in a "dockside community" of unmediated bleakness and despair. The young boy is placed in work by his father, and his first day's work inside the docks is spent baling out the bilges of a ship, standing up to his armpits in fouled water passing up buckets to another young boy at the top of the ladder. Later in the day he is put to work scaling out the inside of the ship's boilers with another team of boys, chipping away in darkness and oppressive heat at the coke deposits left on the boiler walls. As it is his first day the other boys decide he will have to be initiated, a process of being tied up, covered in paint and locked in one of the boilers. Overhearing these plans he runs away and decides on the spot to stow away on another ship about to leave that night. All the other young boys are shown by Hanley to have been rapidly brutalised by the conditions of work and already trapped in a callous and aggressive working-class masculinity.

So the boy hides in the coke-hold of the ship where he quickly becomes very ill and feverish through lack of food, general ill-health and sheer moral terror. He is discovered by one of the seamen who takes him to his cabin, puts the boy to bed and then rapes him. This scene is made all the more powerful by the fact that in the original edition about every third word for the duration of this scene is represented by a series of asterisks. In the morning the captain is notified of the boy's presence and it is agreed that he be allowed to work his passage until the ship returns to England. As the voyage progresses he is bullied and sexually assaulted by a number of members of the crew and his mind becomes increasingly suffused with an enormous horror of life. They arrive at a port in the Middle East for a short stay and the boy is taken by an older sailor to a brothel where the boy becomes infatuated with the young prostitute he is offered. In these novels only prostitutes represent female sexuality. The terrors of

111

adolescent sexuality are again portrayed with power: the rigidities of a particular kind of religious character formation make sexuality, or "lust" as it is most commonly described, a wholly self-destructive desire. The boy contracts syphilis and falls into a violent fever back on board and his mind becomes completely deranged. The captain in a moment of pity goes to him one evening, lays his greatcoat over the boy's face and smothers him to death. The whole action of the novel, from schoolroom to deathbed, takes place within perhaps ten days; and the pace of the novel accelerates as it goes along so that the shock of the boy's death at the end is truly devastating. Such a novel could have been written only by a person who knew life on board ships in all its squalid tyranny and oppressiveness, and by someone who was, as Hanley described himself, "drenched in Strindberg, Synge and Ibsen." One might be more direct and say that *Boy*, has many structural and thematic similarities to Ibsen's *Ghosts*.

In 1935 Hanley published *The Furys*, a long, panoramic saga of working-class family life in Liverpool centred around the Fury family, hence the title. Once again this family, or "workers' dynasty" as Soviet critics came to call this kind of novel, is centred around the whims and wishes of the father, Denny Fury. Denny has been a sailor for most of his life, but has been encouraged to stay at home and oversee the family as they grow into adulthood. Denny feels trapped on land, and, like many other characters in the novels and stories of Hanley, Garrett and Phelan, dreams of taking a ship as a way of escaping the responsibilities and oppressive relationships of everyday social life. Here these writers are looking at certain possibilities of escape from the exigencies of class oppression which the working-class writers of locality and place did not recognise. In *Boy* the young main character had sought escape unsuccessfully in his case — by taking a boat. In *The Furys* Denny is shown early in the novel "floating about the city like a cork upon water, waiting and hoping for some release. Only a ship could deliver him."

Once again the novel focuses on the young son — Peter — who has returned home after a period of some years in Ireland training for the priesthood. He has failed to take Orders, to the enormous disappointment of his mother, who had great hopes of her favourite son becoming a priest, a powerful sentiment in many working-class Catholic families. Peter returns to Liverpool dissatisfied with his life and determined not to get trapped in the way of life of his parents and other brothers and sisters. Peter is the uncommitted observer in the novel, wandering through the bleak and loveless city and through other people's lives as the young Stephen D. wanders through Joyce's *Ulysses*. He witnesses the large demonstrations of the Liverpool unemployed and their brutal suppression by the the police (described at length by George Garrett in *Liverpool 1921-1922* and later by Jim Phelan in *Ten-A-Penny-People*). He is also picked up by the Mephistophelean Professor Titmouse, an ominous and homosexual figure of terrifying visions. He inveigles himself into becoming the lover of his own sister-in-law, an attractive woman estranged from her husband Desmond, an active socialist and railway worker, always out at meetings or at work. Peter inevitably becomes morally corrupted and at the end of the novel runs away to sea to escape the bitter antagonism of the rest of his family whose lives he has betrayed.

The lot of the women in the novel is far worse than that of the men. Mrs Fury is worn out with waiting on the men in the household, including her aged and senile father who, from the beginning of the novel to the end, is always found sitting in the kitchen, strapped to a chair, spoon-fed and speaking gibberish. The kitchen in which the reader always finds Mrs Fury is described in great detail like the dark interior of one of Gorky's peasant homes — a small altar with a candle burning that has been alight for seventeen years, casting a dim flickering light onto the features of the senile old man. At the end Mrs Fury almost gives up eating in order to accelerate the process of her own self-extinction, a woman destroyed by class and sexual oppression. Her last act in the novel is to attack Peter when she finds him about to board ship. She tries to pulp his face which stands for the face of all the men who "had cheated and insulted her".

George Garrett

By the mid 1930s Hanley was getting published regularly in those two important outlets for new writers, particularly those from working-class backgrounds: *Left Review* and John Lehmann's *New Writing*. This was also true of George Garrett. Garrett, like Hanley, was born at the turn of the century into a Liverpool-Irish Catholic family. He went to sea on leaving school, was back in Liverpool to join the 1922 Hunger March to London, went to sea again, travelled around the United States, joined the Wobblies (Industrial Workers of the World), and finally returned to active working-class politics in Liverpool where he remained until his death in 1966. He had a number of stories published in *Left Review* and *New Writing* in 1935-37. "A stoker with a punch," Jim Phelan called him, though a Liverpool priest admired his gentle qualities if not his passionate left-wing politics: "Christlike, though with a bad creed."[6] He set Orwell on the road to Wigan Pier, almost literally, and Orwell remained a great admirer of his writing, as did Sylvia Townshend Warner, who likened his work to that of Defoe.

His story, "Redcap", tells of a ship in a French port during the First World War.[7] The sailors have been forbidden to go ashore and a military policeman (MP) stands on watch to ensure that this order is kept. The hatred of the sailors for this bullying and arrogant figure of authority, keeping them imprisoned on the ship for no real reason, is intense. An older sailor and a younger colleague manage to give the MP the slip one afternoon and get into town to buy some new boots and have a drink. They learn from some British rank-and-file soldiers in town how particularly vicious this MP is. On their return to the boat they are unluckily spotted by the guard who speaks to them with contempt and announces that they will be severely punished. The older man, a veteran of the Boer War and conscious of the way in which working-class people are pushed around in the services and in civilian life, edges the MP towards the wharf edge where he stumbles over a rope and falls into the water. Shouting for help, the MP struggles in the water trying to swim to safety. As if to help him the older man jumps into the water landing deliberately on the MPs head, stunning him and then allowing him to drown. It is a story of terrible frustration and hatred, in which the ending, callous though it seems, also seems inevitable and even just. Garrett, like Hanley, is concerned with extreme circumstances. Thus they write with vivid intensity of people whose consciousness is frequently at fever pitch. Psychological portraiture is of great importance to them.

Another story, "Fishmeal", shows Garrett at his stylistic extremes.[8] This is yet another examination of the terrors of the stoke-hold. In the sailor's quarters the men are grumbling about watch duties. Costain, very much an isolated figure, although ill decides to report for his next shift in the stoke-hold. At work in the heat of the stoking ovens he becomes feverish and mentally deranged. His mind is filled with fantasies of fire and thirst as his body is racked by fever. Suddenly he rushes from the stoke-hold up to the deck screaming and hurls himself into the freezing sea in order to assuage his physical thirst and mental turmoil. A small dinghy is lowered overboard to try to rescue Costain, but he is already dead by the time they reach him. In the process of this rescue another sailor loses the use of both his arms as they are crushed while bringing the small boat back to the side of the larger ship. As the body of Costain is winched aboard, Garrett describes it as hanging like Christ at the Crucifixion. In both the stoke-hold and the wild night sea Garrett paints a picture of utter desolation and extremity.

In June 1936 Garrett also wrote in *The Adelphi* an unusually critical essay on Conrad's *Nigger of the Narcissus*. As an experienced seaman he was in a good position to take Conrad to task for a certain artistic loading of the dice against the character Donkin, Conrad's miserable scapegoat at the centre of that famous story. Garrett brings to his criticism a real understanding of the pressures and material circumstances which force Donkin into the role of an argumentative "sea-lawyer" so despised by Conrad. At a number of key points in the story Garrett challenges Conrad's plausibility in the actual details of seafaring practice. Whereas Conrad invites the reader to identify with the captain and the pride of the ship-owners at the expense of the poorly fed, overworked and miserably paid seamen, Garrett suggests that the reader identifies with the sailors who actually do the work that creates the circumstances for Conrad to write his moral tale.

Looked at in this new light, Conrad's selectivity of material appears artistically damaging. Conrad's final assessment of Donkin is thus: "Donkin, who never did a decent day's work in his life, no doubt earns his living by discoursing with filthy eloquence upon the right of labour to live." Garrett, on the other hand, supports the attitude and character of Donkin on the basis of real experience of the difficulties and tribulations of such a sailor's life. At the end of his essay Garrett looks forward to the day when, "the Donkins might write the story of the sea. Let's hope it will be to better a world in which ship-owners can still send out heavily insured coffin ships and their helpless crews." It is salutary to be reminded that Conrad — much of whose reputation was based on the authenticity of his seaboard settings — should be regarded as quite ignorant of many seafaring matters by sailors themselves. Garrett was not alone among these writers in being critical of Conrad. The narrator in one of Hanley's stories, "Jacob", says that "Conrad was not a sailor, but a writer who happened to go to sea." If there was one fictional creation of sea-going life they all admired, then it was Big Yank, the hero of Eugene O'Neill's expressionist play, *The Hairy Ape*. Big Yank was the obsessed and frenetic stoker *in extremis*. Garrett's first performance as an actor was in a Liverpool WEA production of this O'Neill play.

Garrett also wrote autobiographical reminiscences and descriptions of important political movements in Liverpool in an unpublished work, "Ten Years on the Parish", although the pieces on "The First Hunger March" and *Liverpool 1921-22* were published separately. For some reason he seems to have given up writing at the end of the 1930s, an event which encouraged John Lehmann to write in the first volume of his autobiography, *The Whispering Gallery*, published in 1955:

> If George Garrett, Liverpool seaman and heroic battler against impossible odds, should by any chance read these works, I should like him to know how much I have always regretted that he found it impossible to go on with what he had so vigorously begun; and I should like him to tell me what happened to him.[9]

What happened to him was that the sheer struggle to write in overcrowded conditions, whilst supporting a wife and five children, forced him to give up writing altogether, after having what appears to have been a short physical and mental breakdown.[10]

Jim Phelan

As mentioned before, Garrett and Phelan knew each other and from time to time met when their very circuitous paths crossed, having first met in New Orleans. Phelan was born in a small village outside Dublin in 1895 and first ran away from home when he was three. He ran away for good around the age of eleven and settled for a while in Dublin, working as postboy and living in the anonymity of the slum area known as "The Liberties". He decided to go to sea and eventually, like Garrett, tramped across the United States. In one of his stories, "Happy Ending", the narrator describes the life of a man never at rest: working various passages as a sailor, occasionally meeting up with old friends on different ships, or on casual jobs like grape-picking in France, or living rough in seaports like Marseilles (a city which also fascinated Hanley and provided the setting for his novel *The Closed Harbour*). In his autobiography, *The Name's Phelan*, Phelan writes of his lifelong obsession with flight: "Always, in any danger of difficulty, my immediate impulse is to turn round and head for the horizon." The chronology of Phelan's life is difficult to reconstruct since he never provided any dates in his autobiographical writings. We do know, however, that Phelan had been a member of the Irish Republican Army and was convicted in 1923 for the murder of a man in the course of a post office robbery in Liverpool. Condemned to death, he vividly describes in his autobiography the days he spent in Strangeways prison waiting to be hanged. The death sentence was commuted at the last minute, but he remained in jail until 1937 — a period which is the subject of many reminiscences in *Jail Journey* and *Tramp at Anchor*.

One novel, though, *Ten-A-Penny-People* (1938), perhaps his most sustained work, falls into place quite readily next to the themes and preoccupations of Garrett and Hanley. Published by Gollancz in 1938, it begins in Liverpool with a young boy about to be persuaded by his father to start work on the boats. The opening scene is very similar to those of Hanley's novels and equally powerful. Joe Jarrow (not a very careful disguising of the Joe Jarrett alias George Garrett in the later autobiography) is the young man who refuses his father's place as a trainee stoker on board a ship about to sail, takes on his father in physical combat, and after a brutal slugging match is finally beaten into unconsciousness. Standing over his supine son the father unbuttons his fly and "watered the face of the unconscious boy".[11] Phelan is very much in the same horrendous territory as Hanley. The young boy is taken on board ship where he is immediately befriended by an older sailor known as "Soshie" (the socialist) who gives him a volume of Jack London stories. The novel then quickly moves to a completely different setting with different characters which sets the structure for the rest of the book. For this is a discontinuous succession of scenes and plots, sometimes overlapping and related, sometimes not, as Phelan tries — for the most part successfully — to break away from the determinations of a continuous linear narrative. He thus presents a patchwork of parallel sequences which can be made to represent the simultaneity of working-class life and struggle in various places at the same time. So Joe Jarrow turns up in the novel some years later in another sequence as a tramp.

It is likely that Phelan was very much influenced in his choice of style for this novel by the success of John Sommerfield's *May Day* published two years earlier in 1936, though in prison he had read and been much impressed by Alfred Döblin's epic expressionist novel, *Berlin Alexanderplatz*.[12] Sommerfield's novel itself owed much to the imagery and construction of the documentary film movement of the late 1920s and early 1930s — films like those of Eisenstein and Dovchenko with their dramatic crowd scenes, non-naturalistic lighting, images of individual anguish as well as processions, funerals, work in fields and factories, and villainous kulaks and capitalists. Novels like those of Sommerfield and Phelan owed even more to those documentary films whose aim was to capture the multi-faceted reality of city life, of which Ruttman's *Berlin: Symphony of A City* was the most influential. When the British documentary film-maker John Grierson was describing the imagery of that particular genre of film, the "symphony of the city", he could as well have been describing the techniques of the working-class expressionist writers like Sommerfield, Phelan, Hanley and Garrett:

> The day began with a processional of workers, the factories got under way, the streets filled: the city's forenoon became a hurly-burly of tangled pedestrians and street

119

cars. There was a respite for food: a various respite with contrast of rich and poor. The city started work again, and a shower of rain in the afternoon became a considerable event. The city stopped work and, in futhermore hectic processional of pubs and cabarets and dancing legs and illuminated sky-signs, finished its day.[13]

Phelan's *Ten-A-Penny-People* is built around a number of different incidents which happen at roughly the same time. The opening sections give the formative incidents in the early lives of some of the characters who assume much more important roles later on. Some chapters are prefaced by parts of folk songs or political songs, some by ironic Brechtian interventions. Other sections of the novel are simply snatches of representative kinds of conversations, juxtaposing bits of talk around tea in a working-class household alongside voices of businessmen choosing from the menu in an expensive restaurant. There are central incidents which touch in different ways all of the characters' lives: a strike, a case of arson with murder at the same factory, a failed attempt at suicide by a woman which results in the death of one of her children and a murder charge against her. Some characters know about these things because they are directly involved, others only hear of them as news items.

In some ways Phelan is more successful than Sommerfield in creating believable characters, since Sommerfield as an active communist was more concerned with creating representative (or ideal) types of people who exemplified general psychologies of time and circumstance. Phelan, an anarchist by temperament and self-description, only dealt in generalities of character when he portrayed bosses or party members. There is a strong dislike in the novel for the politically rigid as in his portrayal of one communist couple who can only ever speak in truncated phrases like modern Gradgrinds:

"Interested," explained Dick. "Marvellous reflex-conditioning. Child knows factory really responsible. Works,

120

poverty, tragedy. Marvellous reflexing. Agree?" he inquired, turning to Joan. "Agree," confirmed Joan. "Wages, want, woe-associated. Expressed as 'Poor Ma. The works.' Very striking." "Oh, go to hell, you cold-blooded pair of swine," shouted Kitty, as she dashed from the room.

The Post-war Period

After the Second World War, Phelan published books of autobiographical reminiscence, either about tramping or prison life, and occasionally short stories. Garrett, meanwhile, seems to have had nothing published after the war though he remained politically active in Liverpool. It was Hanley who carried on exploring the possibilities of fiction in a remarkably intense and prolific way. Among those interested in contemporary fiction, Hanley became a writer who from time to time was described as "the greatest living English language novelist"; yet outside such a circle of reviewers his work remains relatively unknown. This is a pity, for he continued to take as the subjects of his novels the very real personal dilemmas of ordinary people and treated these dilemmas and the lives which encompass them with an extraordinary sympathy and insight.

There are several reasons which may explain why Hanley's work has eluded popular attention. First, his novels usually take as their major preoccupation the psychological states of a very small number of characters locked in a very closed world of material circumstances. Little attention is ever paid to the wider society in which these characters live, although their lives are clearly deeply affected by social circumstances. Thus an early post-war novel, *The Closed Harbour* (1952), tells the story of a sea-captain, Marius, stranded with his wife and daughter in Marseilles, as he tries to secure another commission with a shipping company. We learn that something untoward happened on a previous voyage which makes his chances of another situation quite remote, but we never learn what really happened. The main emphasis of the novel is on exploring the obsessive desire of Marius to try to break free of the trap into which he has led himself and his family. His wife and grown daughter, both devout Catholics, regard him with increasing contempt as he wanders each day down to the harbour to try to secure another ship. Marseilles is an overcrowded and corrupt city which breaks its inhabitants either on the wheel of a completely self-denying religion or through the "corruption of the flesh" and desire for power.

The style of writing is intense and highly metaphorical. Faulkner is an acknowledged mentor in Hanley's own development as a writer after 1945. Marius's mind begins to lose touch with reality as the realisation that his life at sea has finished becomes confused with a metaphorical understanding of the decline of shipping. Looking at his old maps and charts, a sympathetic colleague tries to tell Marius that his experience already belongs to a past era, pointing to, "...the seas that had dried up, the ships that lay rotting, the rivers carrying nothing, the lighthouses without lights". At the end Marius finds sanctuary in a hospital for the mentally ill run by a religious order, where everything is peaceful and quiet, but where, in such featureless and institutional surroundings, life had been "levelled flat".

Coming to terms with Hanley's style is not easy. Yet it has to be seen as a very conscious development from the novels and stories of the 1930s in which he usually set his characters in much more naturalistic, dynastic and panoramic working-class settings. Some of his recent novels, published in the 1970s, exemplify both the strengths and weaknesses of Hanley's chosen style. *A Woman in the Sky* (1973) is a small masterpiece of expressionist stream-of-consciousness writing. It concerns a handful of characters living in a tower block on a North London housing estate, especially two elderly women who live together in one flat and their neighbours, an elderly couple next door. Such plot as there is, is precipitated by the suicide of one of the elderly women, a working-class alcoholic, deeply ashamed of having been caught and charged for a shoplifting offence. Hanley uses the incident to explore the inner lives of the remaining woman and her neighbour as they have to cope with this "minor" tragedy. Much of the novel is in speech; either the internal speech of the characters as they shuffle from flat to pub or shopping parade, or between them as they talk about the incident. This speech is often very dense and highly elliptical, but it achieves insights and understandings of the lives that people are driven to negotiate under the pressures of class, material circumstances and emotional difficulty, which one just doesn't find in the contemporary realistic novel.

On the other hand, *A Dream Journey* (1976), about a couple living in London during the war, is tortuously long and much of the writing impenetrable. Hanley makes no concessions to conventional narrative structure and one gets the impression that he never rises from his desk from the first page of the novel until the concluding line. The energy in his writing is amazing but is sometimes defeated by a failure to make any concessions to the need of his readers for moments of recapitulation or exegesis. A subsequent, *A Kingdom* (1978) is more simple and, though not as accomplished as *A Woman in the Sky*, remains a very powerful portrait of two sisters, long estranged, meeting on the death of their father. Again, these are not members of the kind of class which most modern fiction assumes to be the most important — the class to which most writers themselves belong — but people (like Cadi and Lucy in this novel) who work in shops or look after elderly parents on smallholdings in Welsh hill villages. Hanley has said that he is fascinated by the supposedly inarticulate, whose inner minds are actually like "great forests or endless seas".

The Expressionist Mode Today
The achievements of these three novelists are of more than academic interest. For they were writing in a period when

experimentation in cultural forms often went hand in hand with revolutionary ideas in politics. Modernism was more than just an aesthetic movement, it also had political implications. That connection has since the Cold War been completely broken, and revolutionary or radical politics came to be associated with the most dull and unimaginative expectations of what is possible in literature, usually pedestrian verse and prose only distinguished from its "bourgeois" counterparts by the worthiness of its morality.[14]

Garrett, Hanley and Phelan did not try to develop a "proletarian" aesthetic which was independent of the achievements of writers who had emerged — often antagonistically — from more bourgeois cultural backgrounds and traditions. Eclectic in their reading, they were excited and inspired by writers as various as Ibsen, Strindberg, Synge, Joyce, Gorky, O'Neill, Dostoyevsky, Faulkner, Jack London and B. Traven. They were right to think that a new literary aesthetic could not be developed without reference to the achievements of the bourgeois literary tradition which, if critically read and absorbed, could only provide a greater range of styles and techniques for exploring the multi-faceted and complex world of working-class experience.

The material circumstances of their early lives as seamen and itinerants naturally influenced their choice of literary influences and iconography. The era of the great steel transatlantic passenger and cargo ships provided a number of political and experimental writers with the metaphorical images they needed: B. Traven's *Death Ship*, Jack London's *Sea Wolf*, Conrad Aiken's *Blue Voyage*, Malcolm Lowry's *Ultramarine*, O'Neill's *The Hairy Ape* and the transatlantic voyage in Kafka's *America*. Before them, both Melville and Conrad had explored this world of harrowing sea voyages in equally allegorical ways. The Liverpool-Irish writers were fully steeped in this literary tradition. And they also, like many of the writers, together with Gorky, were acquainted with and fascinated by the extraordinary characters found in the most poverty-stricken districts of the world's major cities and seaports. In the various criminal underworlds, in the cafes and bars of the red-light districts, in the sailors' missions and dockside lodging-houses, they saw how many people had tried to find some form of escape or retreat or alternative way of life to that of the factory system. They did not necessarily like or condone what they saw, but they realised it had to be explored.

[1]Walter Benjamin, *Illuminations*, London, 1970, p.84-85. In this essay Benjamin also makes some highly pertinent comments about the decreasing value attributed to the category of personal "experience" by modernising social systems and ideologies.

[2]See Raphael Samuel ed., *People's History and Socialist Theory*, London, 1981, particularly the section on "Local History".

[3]Hilliard describes this desire thoughtfully as a belief in "the transforming power of the revealed truth". Hilliard (2006), p.117.

[4]Jim Phelan, *The Name's Phelan*, London, 1948, p.276.

[5]An excellent study of Hanley's life and work has now been published: John Fordham, *James Hanley: Modernism and the Working Class*, University of Wales Press, Cardiff, 2002.

[6]The brief biographical notes about Garrett by Jerry Dawson, are contained in "Liverpool 1921-1922", Whitechapel Press, Liverpool, undated.

[7]George Garrett, "Redcap", *Left Review*, October 1935.

[8]George Garrett, "Fishmeal", *New Writing*, Autumn 1936.

[9]John Lehmann, *The Whispering Gallery*, London, 1955.

[10]Garrett's difficult writing circumstances are well documented in Hilliard (2006), p.105-106.

[11]Pissing on the face of a defeated victim as an act of final humiliation occurs in one of Hanley's most famous stories, "The German Prisoner", seized and destroyed by the police in 1930, and re-published in *London Magazine*, February/March 1996, Vol. 35, Nos 11 & 12.

[12]I owe this new information to a short essay on Phelan's work by Paul Lester: "Lifer: The Writings of Jim Phelan", *London Magazine*, Vol. 36, Nos 7 & 8, October/November 1996.

[13]*Grierson on Documentary*, London, 1979, p. 39-40.

[14]For an excellent range of debates about the connection between radical politics, class and writing, see the full run of *Voices* magazine discussed earlier.

Out of the Ghetto: The Literature of London's Jewish East End

It is one of the paradoxes of writing that the act of representing the life of the community in which the writer has grown up is often the first step by which the working-class writer is separated from that life, often forever. At the same time as many people acquire their first typewriter, they also acquire their first suitcase.[1] The two are often connected. They might also feel a pressure to remove themselves in order to write: to another district or to London, somewhere known as a place for "writing" — Grub Street, Bloomsbury, Soho, Hampstead — as if the air were more conducive to writing and varied from postal district to postal district, and thrived at least better in a capital city.

Jewish East London, between the 1890s and the beginning of the Second World War in 1939, has been sufficiently mythologised in showbusiness reminiscences, the ghosted autobiographies of dance-band leaders and boxers, as well as a number of detailed Communist Party memoirs, for it to be acknowledged that a quite singular and complex cultural milieu was created in that period whose richness and vitality is still almost tangible to this day. That culture produced many writers, and I want to look at the work of three of them. Between them they produced over a dozen novels and collections of short stories between 1934 and 1945 whose starting points were almost exclusively situated in Jewish working-class life in London's East End. The three writers are Simon Blumenfeld, Willy Goldman and Ashley Smith.

Nearly all of their work has been long out of print, which is a great pity, since much of it provides a valuable corrective to subsequent romanticisation of that era, written as it was directly out of experience rather than recollected in maturity and restructured in the light of the meaning of the lives they later came to lead. For when people look back they often impose a meaning on the past to convince themselves that events took a natural direction, were ordained in some way and that things could not have happened in any other way. Those writing at the time gazed into a completely uncertain future in which at times they thought anything was possible and at other times thought that nothing was possible at all.

Right from the early days of settlement by Jewish immigrants in East London, at the end of the nineteenth century, the task of establishing the community's own religious and cultural institutions began. Synagogues were either built new, or adapted from existing buildings. The synagogue in Brick Lane was in earlier times a Huguenot church. Today it is a mosque. The political tradition described in Bill Fishman's *East End Jewish Radicals*, particularly the secular and anarchist clubs, were a direct influence on many young Jewish workers who through them came into contact not only with the world of ideas and opinions, but also with the worlds of music, literature, art and the theatre. The Workers' Friend Club opened in Jubilee Street on 3 February 1906 was the home of an enormous range of activities, as Fishman describes:

> Much of the cultural activity, initiated by (the anarchist Rudolf) Rocker, centred on the stage. Here, almost inclusively in the *mame loshen*, took place lectures, concerts, recitations, sketches (sometimes written by the performers themselves concerning current labour themes) and plays — classical and modern. Sam Goldenberg, erstwhile tailor turned star of the international Yiddish theatre, learned his stage-craft in the club, where he was seen by "Red" Rose performing as a young amateur in Andreiev and sketches of Sholem Aleichem. Here young Leftwich watched rehearsals of a Yiddish production of Ibsen's *Ghosts* and observed the making of the future maestro of Shakespearean theatre, Abraham Teitelbaum, on the same boards. Friday... was lecture night. Speakers would include Rocker, Tchekesov, Kaplan, Kropotkin, and

Malatesta, on subjects ranging from world literature and science to modern political ideologies...[2]

The Yiddish Theatre in Commercial Road was frequented by young political activists and writers. Isaac Rosenberg was a regular theatre-goer before the First World War; the writers of the 1930s also reflected their familiarity with this theatre tradition in their short stories and novels. A third significant centre in the cultural life of Jewish East London was the Whitechapel Library where, under the supervision of a Mr Bogdin for more than forty years, young Jews came to read, talk and educate themselves.[3] Both Rosenberg, the poet, and the painters Mark Gertler and David Bomberg regularly used this library: Rosenberg autographed a copy of his early poems for Bogdin.[4] Another Whitechapel librarian, Morley Dainlow, introduced Rosenberg to the work of a number of Victorian poets — Tennyson, Browning and Swinburne, certainly — as well as writing comments on Rosenberg's own first attempts at poetry. Blumenfeld, Goldman and Smith all mention the library at least once in their various fictional and autobiographical writings. The worker-poet, Julius Lipton, a tailor's presser, had his collection *Poems of Strife* published in 1935 and noted in the frontispiece that the poems were "Written in the Whitechapel Reference Library".[5]

The important role this particular library played in many young Jewish workers' lives is worth emphasising. For much of the 19th century, radical politics espoused and created its own institutions — meeting halls, libraries, co-operatives, even communes. At the end of the 19th century many of those forms were absorbed into the civic culture of local government — or displaced. Once the labour movement embraced parliamentarianism that record of self-organisation was largely abandoned. In the 1930s, however, the Communist Party was admirably active in re-creating that tradition through such projects as the various Unity theatres, and more specific bodies such as the Workers' Film Movement, the Workers' Theatre Movement and its choirs, orchestras and other cultural networks.

In East London, though, a separate and active, self-contained and relatively autonomous culture of the Jewish working-class existed well into the 1930s, a kind of culture which had for the most part disappeared elsewhere, except for the mining villages of South Wales and parts of northeast England and Scotland — the "Little Moscows" of Stuart MacIntyre's excellent study.[6] It is no coincidence that it is mostly these areas of political militancy which produced the most successful working-class writers of the period. Thus Lewis Jones, Idries Davies and B.L. Coombes writing in South Wales; Walter Allen, Leslie Halward and Walter Brierley as the "Birmingham Group"; Garrett, Hanley and Phelan in Liverpool; Jack Lawson and Jack Common from Tyneside. A strong sense of being outside conventional cultural patterns and routines not surprisingly characterises these writers and their work. But in many ways the Jewish writers in East London were more prolific than the writers from other regions, even though they were all writing about the one small district, whose intricacies of life and politics were never exhausted.

Simon Blumenfeld

Simon Blumenfeld's *Jew Boy* was the first of the autobiographical novels to appear from this group of writers and was published in 1935.[7] The novel concerns two young East London working-class Jews, Alec and Dave, both in their early twenties, trying to make some choices about their futures out of the despair and hopelessness which they find around them. Alec inclines towards creating a distinctive Jewish socialist politics, whereas Dave is obsessed with sexual conquest and seems to spend his waking life pursuing this objective. One might well be the alter ego of the other. Alec's critique of the way in which radical Jewish culture is becoming diffused and fragmented is the most important motif of the novel and gives

130

it some real weight as historical testimony. The old culture is losing its relevance. Alec and Dave still occasionally go to the Workers' Circle club in Alie Street (the building still exists) to listen to the Sunday concerts of Beethoven and Brahms, mostly attended by an ageing generation of anarchists reading *Freiheit*. On the other hand, they see no serious future in the path represented by a number of younger Jews who are portrayed as trying to resurrect a rather anachronistic Jewish folk literature (presumably going back to the novelist Israel Zangwill as their mentor). At a party Alec has a book of poems thrust into his hand by the leading member of this school, called Leopold Hartmen, and reacts thus:

> I glanced through his masterpiece *Songs from the High Hills*. That was enough for me. There really isn't anything Jewish about Hartmen's work, or for that matter the work of almost any Jewish writer, writing in English. They're fakers, exhibitionists, poseurs, almost to a man. None of them paints a truthful picture of the Jew as he really is. In England, at any rate, there aren't any more of their pet Jews left, with snotty beards, and greasy kaftans. Their characters are horribly sentimentalised: the "Vichs", and "Vots" and "Schadchans" are laid on with trowels.

For Alec, class is as important as religion. Throughout the novel he is searching for an alternative way of life to that of the old culture, which is crumbling. He visits an old school friend who has moved out into the suburbs, and who now leads the life of the "progressive" middle class. His bitter summary of the political ineffectiveness of this group — which must have made rather uncomfortable reading at the time, given the esteem with which this class regarded itself — is one of the most powerful sections of the book. Left on his own for a few minutes he surveys the bookshelves:

> Amongst others, Warwick Deeping, Ethel Mannin, David Gamett, Arthur Symons. Several Shakespeares... a

Dickens set (probably from the *Daily Mail*)... Bernard Shaw... H.G.Wells... Macaulay... Professors Lodge and Jeans... A fat Nuttall's dictionary... Fowler's Modern English Usage...

Just what he might have expected. A catholic taste. Quite conventional middle-class, even to the ready-made guides to the universe, handy keys to the problems of the eternal wheres and whyfores. A whole library of escape. You only had to pick up one of these books, and your mind soared into the vast empyrean, and you forgot there were such mundane things on earth as unemployment queues for example, and labour colonies, and filthy East End slums.

Alec meets a prostitute (who in many novels in this period are the only emotionally and economically independent women, particularly in working-class communities) and settles down with her. This is his most decisive break with his family and cultural tradition, to live with and possibly marry a *shiksa*, a non-Jewish woman. They get on well until the inevitable happens — an unwanted pregnancy — and this is terminated by an abortion that is as harrowing psychologically as it is physically.

Here is a second key issue that characterises many of the most influential novels of working-class life since the 1930s: the unwanted pregnancy and, in most cases, the subsequent illegal abortion. More than any other detail of working-class life, the illegal abortion is a kind of set-piece in such novels, marking the bitterest point of disillusionment and helplessness, much more so than any episode to do with work. The spectre of an unwanted pregnancy haunts the novels of Blumenfeld and Goldman. Sillitoe's *Saturday Night and Sunday Morning*, Bill Naughton's *Alfie*, Nell Dunn's *Up the Junction* and more recently Pat Barker's *Union Street* all make such traumatic abortions central incidents in their narratives. The main theme of Stan Barstow's novel, *A Kind of Loving*, was the ill-advised rush into marriage occasioned by the woman's pregnancy. And even though some of these writers were not themselves working-class, it is significant that their portraits of working-class life naturally included this central fact of fear of pregnancy and the presence of the illegal abortionist in working-class communities.

Alec is increasingly drawn into trade-union and left-wing politics, and the novel concludes with him vowing to dedicate his life to the cause of international working-class politics. The break is made from religion into politics. Alec finds his cultural identity in the struggle for socialism. Blumenfeld's *Jew Boy* (the title was deliberately assertive) was, according to Joe Jacobs in his posthumously published memoir of East London communist politics *Out of the Ghetto* based on a rather singular Communist Party militant called Sam Berks, a widely known and admired figure in East London whose popularity was possibly connected with his ability to be fairly sanguine about party orthodoxy while remaining steadfastly active. "I want Communism without Communists", was one of his memorable aphorisms.

In retrospect Blumenfeld's subsequent work seems to lack direction — the problem his main character worried about so much in his first novel. The next novel was a large-scale story of three generations, *Phineas Kahn: Portrait of an Immigrant*. The novel opens with the young Phineas in flight from the pogroms in Russia, first to Holland and then to London. He settles in Whitechapel, marries, fathers ten children, lives through various domestic tragedies and at the end of the novel returns to Russia, where his oldest daughter has gone to settle after the Revolution. It is a competently written novel, but with so many characters there is no real thematic development: it is simply the story of a large family and their tribulations. East London life only occasionally impinges on the lives of the characters.[8]

Phineas Kahn was followed a year later by *Doctor of the Lost*, a fictional reconstruction of Dr Barnardo's life. Technically competent though it is, it fits strangely into a highly conventional and received tradition of seeing the East End working-class as an abject and pitiful teeming mass, denizens of a nether world, who are only capable of being rescued from drunkenness and squalor by individual philanthropists and welfare agencies directed from without. Another year later *They Won't Let You Live* came. A rather programmatic left novel, it is built around a number of representative "types", as in an updated morality play: the rich West End money-lender, the poor but honest working-class woman whom in earlier life he had got pregnant and abandoned, a Cockney taxi driver who embodies all that is good and honest, a local fascist leader and a number of other part players. Yet there are times when the novel really comes alive and grips the reader with the passion with which some of the scenes were clearly felt and re-created by the writer.

In *They Won't Let You Live*, Blumenfeld reminds us of two particular kinds of pressure, one economic, the other cultural, which bit deeply into the community life of the Jewish East End and threatened many families with the real possibility of economic and social disintegration. The first was the plight of the small shopkeeper, insufficiently capitalised to survive in a vicious system of larger chain stores and more intense credit squeezes. This plight may seem of little interest to those who would wholly base a definition of class around industrial, "organised" workers, but it has to be remembered that in the Jewish East End political ideologies of socialism could, even had to, coexist with the world of small workshop production and family businesses.

Socialist politics within the Jewish community was fired by terrible material poverty as well as a means of combating the anti-Semitism of populist rightwing groupings. So, whereas in other Labour strongholds shopkeepers and small businessmen might have been expected to sit as Conservative councillors, in East London within memory many such people have sat — and been effective — as leftwing Labour councillors or even Communists.

In *They Won't Let You Live* two obviously sympathetic characters are driven to suicide as credit companies foreclose on them and force them into bankruptcy. Other lives are threatened by a different kind of insidious economic dissipation — gambling. There are moments of genuine tension in the novel as characters in financial extremes gamble what little they have left in the hope of being able to win back sufficient money to start repaying debts to corner shops, or to buy a roll of cloth that can be tailored into suits for another month's economic survival. The temptation, of course, in a world of small businesses was to "borrow" money from the till for the last desperate gamble. The gambling underworld of bookmakers, street runners, billiard saloons, card schools in cafes, dog-track meetings was an ever-present abyss into which the Jewish male characters could fall. And in this novel Blumenfeld reminds us of something very real and often very destructive within that culture which has tended to be forgotten. The worst thing that could happen in many Jewish families was for a son to slip into the gambling network and become a "lowlife".

Paradoxically, much of the ebullience and profligacy that people recall in the Jewish East End at this time reflects a degree of inter-penetration with the criminal underworld — which also had its political and aesthetic predilections. To be interested in writing did not necessarily mean that a young working-class Jew had to be uninterested in gambling, boxing, or, of course, radical politics. The best direct autobiographical account of the richness of this pre-war cultural milieu is that of Joe Jacobs in his account of his teenage years as a member of the Young Communist League in Stepney:

> I was getting to know more of East London as distinct from my East End. We were meeting dockers, seamen, municipal workers, builders, transport workers and so on, through the many TU and Labour organisations right through the area. This linked up with similar activities on an all-London scale. I was soaking up all I could read. It started with books like *The Ragged Trousered Philanthropists*, through to almost everything written by

Upton Sinclair, Jack London, John Dos Passos, Romain Rolland, Mann, Remarque, Ibanez, Tolstoy, Gorky and so on. Then there came William Morris, Robert Owen, H.G. Wells, Arnold Bennett, J.B. Priestley. We got to know them all. Then there was the heavy stuff. It started with sections from Marx, published in pamphlet form — *Value, Price and Profit*; *Wage Labour and Capital*. There was the *Communist Manifesto*, great works I thought. Eventually, we went on to tackle *Capital* in full.[9]

It is interesting to note that English writers form very much a secondary list in the reading that he mentions — one thing that an internationalist political perspective engendered was an interest in writers from other countries. Jacobs then goes on to describe at length the Workers' Educational Association Classes at Toynbee Hall — where an anti-fascist militant such as Alexander Hartog attended opera-singing classes that subsequently dominated his life — with lectures by well-known intellectuals such as Brailsford, Laski and G.D.H. Cole.[10] Jacobs also attended the Yiddish Theatre in Whitechapel Road, the British Workers' Sports Federation based at the Alie Street Workers' Circle Club, and keenly followed the careers of the great Jewish boxers such as Ted Kid Lewis, Jack Kid Berg, Harry Mason and Al Phillips. He also loved the local music halls: "The Paragon on the Mile End Road, as well as the Olympia and the London were my favourite haunts." This rich milieu was not restricted to the Jewish community: boxer-poets and docker-poets could also be found in the non-Jewish community too.[11]

In the course of all of these activities Jacobs met and courted a young woman called Pearl who, he found out, "at one time was going steady with a chap called Willie Goldman who later wrote *East End My Cradle*. He had a friend, whose name escapes me, who fancied himself to be a poet. They seemed quite nice people and they all formed part of a wide circle of Young Communists who seemed to use the 'Circle House' as a base for their activities."

Willy Goldman[12]

It was Willy Goldman's *East End My Cradle* which proved to be the most successful attempt to capture this extraordinary period in writing as it happened. This autobiography had been fairly long in the making, and parts of it had already appeared as short "documentary" stories in John Lehmann's *New Writing*. It is undisguised autobiography reconstructed with great passion and literary adroitness. In a short time it became the best well-known book about the Jewish East End and it remains the one that people still remember today, even among those who remember few others.

For the teenage Goldman family life was experienced as oppressive and restrictive:

> Parents here never have any problems about a son's future. It's all fixed at the cradle. There's only one small detail to think of: shall it be "ladies" work or "gents"?

The garment industry, or "rag trade", was a major industry in East London, as it is today, though worked by a different generation of immigrant workers. Goldman tells of a young man who resists the pressures to conform to family and neighbourhood expectations, without really knowing what it is that he wants from life, like Alec in Blumenfeld's *Jew Boy*. And so he recounts the different kinds of possibilities that presented themselves to him and his other male friends in their adolescent years. The world of billiard halls and boxing clubs is one such possibility and Goldman evokes this — and the territorial and gang violence which they engendered — with a frightening realism. Subsequent accounts of this era have tended to gloss over the reality of Jewish involvement in the razor gangs, the gambling clubs and the race-track mobs, though it certainly existed.

Similarly, adolescent sexuality and its frustrations are shown to be traumatic. In Goldman's account it was the common thing for adolescent boys to be sexually initiated by local older women, often the mothers of known school friends who could no longer ply their trade as prostitutes in the West End or even compete in the East End pubs. In addition, of course, there were real infatuations that could be followed by strained courtships — often assiduously promoted by the families of the young people involved — pushing inexorably towards marriage and lifelong domesticity. *East End My Cradle* describes this restricting side of Jewish East London well.

Yet the main theme of Goldman's first book, a theme that subsequently runs through all his later work, is the sense of becoming an outsider to the inherited family and neighbourhood culture, largely through the wish to become a writer. Of all the working-class writers of the 1930s and post-war years, Goldman is the most consistent explorer of this fault-line: that between the working-class writer and the community from which they come (and which in turn becomes the subject-matter of their writing).

For though writers might regard themselves as chroniclers, folklorists or amanuenses, those written about could come to see them as collaborators or spies. Though this applied particularly to writers, it also applied to those who were not prepared to follow past traditions and wanted to make a future for themselves, independently. Goldman also writes at length about the tragedy of his school friend Wise, who he meets again several years later in the Whitechapel Library reading room. By this time Wise is set on the idea of developing his talent as a painter, an ambition bitterly resented by his family. Goldman recounts:

> To his people he was a "problem" but not a psychological one. He was merely the problem of the "no-good". That was their explanation of his artistic ambitions. He was "too big for his boots". They felt he had no right to be "different". People with warped lives will forgive you anything but being different from themselves.

Wise manages to get into art school but finds that he can't afford the fees, which his family refuse to pay. No support is forthcoming once he decides to break away from the family expectation that he should follow everybody else into the tailoring trade. So he becomes a drifter, sleeping rough or occasionally in one of the "Rowton Houses", rapidly deteriorating in health and mental well-being. Within a year of their meeting up again, Wise has died of "Delirious Mania and Exhaustion" in Colney Hatch Asylum. It is the bitterest moment in Goldman's chronicle, and elicits the savagely critical judgement that,

> That is why my birthplace will always draw me at the same time that it saddens me; there, in that little graveyard of human hopes lie their murdered aspirations...

Goldman goes on to talk about his own aspirations to be a writer, and in his account of his own struggle to find both a form and style to match the political passion of his own sense of injustice, he raises issues that are still relevant today: how to create enduring literature out of what begins as politics. Even his own attempt to describe the problem of avoiding over-writing and the too ready employment of clichés, exemplifies the matter:

> One night when sleep became difficult for the hunger gnawing in my stomach and the strange tumult in my head, I dressed and went out into the cold grey streets of East London's dockside. I saw the wretches huddled in doorways and ragged prostitutes slinking by walls, and I wept at their misery and my own. There arose in me at the same time the desire to scream the story of our common fate into the face of the world. It soon took me like a fever, and I tramped towards home with my hunger forgotten in the ecstasy of a new-found resolution.
>
> I sat down at my table and wrote without pause. I wrote what I had seen. It was not a story — it was a statement. Tears again flowed down my face as I re-lived the experience on paper, but they must have been tears engendered by self-pity, for when I re-read what I had written next day I was unable to recapture my original emotion... I was

made miserable by the futility involved in continually producing masterpieces at night that showed up as
counterfeits in the morning.

East End My Cradle ends with Goldman beginning to earn
small sums of money for articles and receiving a
favourable reader's comment on a novel he had submitted
to a London publisher. As a writer, he concludes, he has
made a start in life.

The next book of Goldman's to be published (unlike
Blumenfeld's books, there seems to be no relationship in
Goldman's work between when books were written and
the order in which they were published, which makes
reading them as a developing body of work difficult if not
impossible), *The Light in the Dust*, which came out in
1944, is certainly not the novel mentioned in *East End My
Cradle*. Instead it is a curious work claiming in the introduction to be based on the diary of another young East
End Jewish writer who killed himself and whose papers
and notes came into Goldman's hands. Internal evidence
suggests strongly that this was a stylistic device, and that
the character is Goldman himself, whose own early life
and political involvements are very much those recorded
in the "diary".

However, it is certainly true that a young would-be writer
known to Goldman killed himself around this time. This we
learn from Maurice Levinson's autobiography, *The Trouble
With Yesterday* published in 1946.[13] Although not directly
mentioning Goldman, Levinson talks about going to
Communist Party meetings with a Max and a Willy, and
also spending time at the Whitechapel Library with the
same pair. Willy is almost certainly Goldman himself and
Alex may well have been Goldman's friend Wise. In
Levinson's book Max dies young of malnutrition and poor
health, though Levinson mentions another young man
whom called Stukey, a writer known to them all, who killed
himself at the age of twenty-two. So it is likely that
Goldman based *The Light in the Dust* on a real event.

140

The image of the writer in this period — a trope employed by so many East End writers — is that of a doomed Keatsian hero, innately talented, scorned by those around him and pre-ordained to sacrifice his health and sanity in the quest to describe some final truth about life and experience. The pervasiveness of this received idea meant that in practice these young writers did sit writing into the night in solitude, unsupported by the companionship of other writers and political friends, and that they saw their project as one of producing a completely personal testimony, which had to be achieved in spite of other people rather than in common cause with them. Made to feel isolated because they wrote, they then isolated themselves further in the cause of writing. Here is the anonymous diarist writing about the effects of first getting published:

> I have recently had my first two short pieces published in a Socialist literary monthly. This fact has not changed my social or economic status in the least. In a certain sense it has even had an adverse effect on me socially; the family now suspects what I am up to. The monthly is sold in a local bookshop, so others besides the family have discovered about my literary activities. The general notion, I gather, is that perhaps I am a queer guy, not like themselves, perhaps nasty even. "If he's got brains, why not go in for something healthy and normal, like a crossword puzzle or picking winners?"

The writer goes on to recall a life, on leaving school, mostly spent at the Whitechapel Library reading room. He describes his unenthusiastic membership of "the Party", with whose literary magazine he feels himself to be in total disagreement, and final months spent in the unsatisfying company of middle-class *literati*, drinking in pubs in and around Leicester Square. This last period was not incidental for it anticipated the general drift of East London writers to Charlotte Street and Soho after the war, which had significant implications both for the writers and the community they left behind. One last quote from this book seems to represent Goldman's literary aesthetic, which is worth recording:

> My position now is that though I am still preoccupied by what is called "ordinary life" as a subject matter, I am against the bare recording reporting method which is considered its natural form. Such a method leaves unexpressed those valuable aspects of fantasy and lyricism which, for me, exist as an integral part of all life, no matter its "ordinariness". The edict that literature is "life seen through a temperament" seems to me as a truth indestructible and permanent...[14]

Goldman's next published novel, *A Tent of Blue*, was the story of a marriage. Again, the opening sections had already appeared some years before in Lehmann's *New Writing*. In the early part of the novel two young "rag trade" workers, Lotte and Ben, meet and conduct a light-hearted courtship that results, inevitably, in Lotte's pregnancy. This is well done. The wedding, which is hastily arranged by both families, is felt by the couple as on occasion more like a funeral, the beginning of a domesticity they didn't want to enter into so young, marking the end of a small era of personal freedom which had hardly begun. So Goldman makes the wedding ceremony and party a ghastly parody of a celebration in which everybody in turn weeps and laughs, dances and sings, whilst the couple themselves sit in the midst of all the gaiety, numb and frozen inside. The early months of marriage and the birth of the first child all happen within a relationship that is already routinised and emotionally dead.

By accident Ben becomes involved in a young Jewish theatre group, which meets in a room above the offices of the Bakers' Union, and in doing so he becomes involved with more politically and sexually independent Jews of his own age. Politics becomes his point of self-identity too. The novel ends with Ben's election as branch secretary of his union in the garment trade and in a mood of self-achievement he promises to try to make his marriage work. *A Tent of Blue* is rather broken-backed in that the first half, which deals with sexual and familial oppression, is well handled, whereas the second half becomes rather formulaic, and at odds with the psychological narrative of the first part. In the same year that A *Tent of Blue* was published, Goldman also had another novel published, *Some Blind Hand*, a lifeless, geographically and culturally unlocated novel about a handful of young writers who agonise about their spiritual calling as such and spend their time hanging around the offices of publishers' agents and reviews editors, trying to pick up odds and ends of paid literary work. The novel seems to epitomise the crisis involved in the movement from a known and lived locality and culture, as the East End was for such writers as Goldman, to the cultural idiosyncrasy and anomie of Soho and Fitzrovia, a move that was made by many writers in this period.

Some Blind Hand is a novel describing how difficult it is to write a novel — a sure sign that a writer has nothing left to say. Raymond Williams who had reason to be in and out of Soho in the late 1940s, when he and Wolf Mankowitz established *Politics and Letters* there, described this cultural crisis when writing about the ethos of the literary magazines in that period, particularly Cyril Connolly's *Horizon*:

> The peculiar tone of much thirties culture — descended from the Bloomsbury ethos — found its final expression in this magazine of the forties: above all, an extreme subjectivism, projecting personal difficulties of being a writer as central social problems.[15]

The same problem reappears in Goldman's next novel, *The Forgotten Word*, published in 1948. The narrator, Harry, who changes his name to Vincent in the pursuit of his literary career, finds lodgings with a middle-class couple. He spends most of his time pursuing sexual affairs in various parts of London and worrying about how difficult it is to be a writer. The notion of becoming a writer, by which the emphasis moves from the activity itself to some generic concept of the person who does it — or in the case of several of Goldman's characters, doesn't — has by this time become one of the most self-destructive tropes of contemporary fiction.

Vincent readily accepts a commission to ghost-write the memoirs of an elderly doctor who would like his life's fund of amusing anecdotes recorded for posterity. Towards the end of the novel, and once again in urgent need of money, Vincent writes to a sex-manual publisher offering his services as a copy-writer. The main thing, it seems, is still to be able to call oneself a writer. It is likely that these last two novels were actually written during the war itself. The fact that Goldman could write two novels at this time without mentioning the war shows exactly how encompassing this literary solipsism was, and that the ideology of subjectivism could so easily blind writers to the catastrophes going on in the wider world.

Goldman published two more books at the beginning of the 1950s, a collection of short stories, *A Saint in the Making*, and another novel, *A Start in Life*. Both return to the world Goldman knew and wrote best about — the Jewish East End. The short stories are often revised and rewritten episodes from earlier books fashioned into more self-contained pieces. The novel is a serious portrait of a family and of how the son Yasha drifts away into the underworld and, once again, finds himself in the comradeship of socialist politics. One particular story in *A Saint in the Making* called "There's heredity close behind me" is worth quoting. It alludes to the suspicion with which the activity of writing was regarded by Goldman's family and neighbourhood. A short story about four brothers who all share a dislike of work, the narrator concludes:

> We find we're rather proud of this. Especially as we've improved on my father's loafing by giving our own more

subtlety. My brothers, who are in the clothing trade, unfortunately still have to do a great deal of work from time to time. But they claim, proudly, that I, who am a "writer", have brought the family tradition of loafing to its logical conclusion.

It's the funniest sentence in the story and the most bitter. Few writers have explored how the activity of writing itself can so easily lead to self-pity and even self-destruction, as Goldman did.

Ashley Smith

Ashley Smith's published work is very different from that of Blumenfeld or Goldman. Another Jewish East Ender, the characters in his short stories and novels are largely the non-Jewish working-class. His first book was a collection of short stories, *Children With Fire*, and was published in 1934 when he was only 26. The stories for the most part, though about working-class people, are written within an aesthetic and literary tradition which is not that of Blumenfeld or Goldman. Rather he has adopted the aesthetics of the short stories of Joyce's *Dubliners* or Katherine Mansfield's *Bliss*, where the luminousness and momentariness of the atmosphere and mood created by the narrative is the most important part of the story. There is usually one principal character at the centre of each of these stories — a boxer who has failed to make the grade and becomes a "has-been" at the age of twenty-one, an elderly and lonely social worker coming to the end of her career helping others, a young boy crippled in a street accident, a local beauty queen struck down by consumption — whose hopes have been extinguished by some arbitrary act of fate. The book was dedicated, as was common certainly for most first novels or collections of short stories by working-class writers in the 1930s, to a patron, Geoffrey West, who might well have been the same dedicatee as the G.W. of Maurice Levinson's *The Trouble With Yesterday*.

In 1937 Ashley Smith's first novel, *The Brimming Lake*, was published, a story of a working-class family in which the husband is a rather impractical kind of socialist dreamer — a shopkeeper — who moves his family from the north-east of England to East London to start a new life after their shop fails. Although the main part of the story concerns the young son Terry's growth into adulthood and political and sexual awareness, Ashley Smith gives the subsidiary characters important episodes of their own so that the novel is more than just the story of a singular development. The author is also concerned with the disjunction between the failed shopkeeper Hegarty's political idealism and activity, and his simultaneous total disregard for his oppression of his own wife, Deirdre. The family begins to disintegrate towards the end of the novel as Hegarty drinks more heavily while Deirdre becomes obsessed with preventing her son Terry from marrying "below himself". Terry becomes resigned to settling down locally and blending into the life around him. The disintegration of the family is halted only by Deirdre's self-sacrifice when she deliberately becomes pregnant again and subsequently dies in childbirth, leaving Hegarty and Terry to build their world anew for the baby whose birth releases in them new energies and dreams.

You Forget So Quickly (1946) provides a sequel. It deals with the effects of the Munich crisis of 1938 on a small group of office workers in East London, several of whom we have met before in *The Brimming Lake*. Technically the book is more formalist in that it incorporates some of the documentary techniques employed by other left novelists in the late 1930s, as in John Sommerfield's *May Day* and Jim Phelan's *Ten-A-Penny-People*. It is divided into seven chapters, one for each day of the week. Each day represents the story of one of the characters, with the others playing subsidiary roles on that day. (Pat Barker's early novel *Union Street* employed the same technique.) The prospect of war looms like a dark cloud over the characters' lives, and they all react differently. Some choose active opposition to the war, others adopt pacifism, some turn to jingoism and militarism, others to drink. The least likeable characters scheme to find a safe place in the Civil Defence bureaucracy. The book ends with news of Chamberlain's return from Munich and the office relaxes back into its old parochial optimism.

In between his first novel and its sequel in 1939, Ashley Smith had a book published called *A City Stirs*, an impressionistic account of twenty-four hours in the life of London, very much in the genre of the "symphony of the city" which was developed in the 1930s. Elsewhere, I have tried to show how this literary genre was, I believe, developed by left-wing writers from the documentary film movement, particularly Ruttman's Berlin: *Symphony of a City*.[16] The aesthetic strategy of this genre was to show the multiplicity of experience in the life of the modern city, and by contrasting the lives of the rich and the poor to arouse a consciousness of contradiction and contrast.

A City Stirs has no plot, and is formally divided into twelve chapters beginning with "Midnight" and ending with "Late Night Final", and it reveals all of the difficulties of appropriating a form developed in one aesthetic mode (film) and using it for another (literature) without modification, or any other kind of mediation. The task of translating visual images into words is often difficult enough (these are often the bits readers skip), but when this is done for an unbroken length of one hundred and fifty pages, communication breaks down completely. One paragraph gives some indication of just how dense such writing is and how inevitably self-defeating; even though the individual paragraphs have much merit and style:

> The controllers in power stations watch the rising chart as office lights are switched on for the charwomen to make their salutary rounds. In gas stations the levels fall as housewives cook their morning meals. In Threadneedle Street and Lombard Street baize-aproned caretakers are polishing brass nameplates. The conductor arms of trams are being swung, fizzling with electric sparks as they

reach the wires overhead. The sleeping men on the cafe floors have disappeared like melting snow. The trains have carried the night workers to their odd daytime beds. Newsboys are beginning to call the morning papers. They run along with an air of bewilderment as they snatch at their creased sheets — as if they were conscious of a falsity, prophesying and informing so confidently at this early onset of a young day. The tide is not yet in, but they are telling the depth of the wave. The houses stand out in their sharpest silhouettes. The light is enough to show quite dearly the lines of their roofs and walls, but not strong enough to confuse the grey stones of its own brightness. Council roadmen are spreading sand on sloping roads, sweeping their heaped shovels with wide movements, as if they were scything grass. Belted busmen are hurrying to their depots, their ticket-punches in tin boxes under their arms.

Certainly there is movement here, and historical evocation, but to the contemporary reader it must have been hard work, not made any easier by the conscious alliteration of the language and the prolixity of the detail. Reading it now in small episodes, as one might read Mayhew's journalism, it is powerful and occasionally hypnotic. At the time it was must have been considered a bold, but in the end unsuccessful, piece of technical experimentalism.

From the East End to Soho
In Goldman's work, the emigration at the end of the 1930s from East London to Soho seems almost obligatory. The move was as symbolic culturally as it was geographically. For not only did it involve a change of address, it also involved a change in aesthetics and literary ideology. Many writers who made this move stopped writing about the communities they came from, and instead started writing about eccentrics, losers, and thwarted writers like themselves.

There had always been a strong connection between Soho and the East End, as Soho also had a small but thriving Jewish community from the beginning of the century. As Chaim Lewis in *A Soho Address* wrote: "Soho had its thriving ghetto in the spacious decades before the First World War. It was to some extent Whitechapel's overspill into the West End."[17]

Chaim Lewis remembered at least five synagogues in Soho during his childhood and adolescence — he was born in 1911 — and even a "Christian Mission to the Jews". Soho had been a centre of cosmopolitanism since the middle of the nineteenth century and was the first home of many political refugees and exiles. Marx lived there for a while and, as Stan Shipley demonstrated in his excellent *Club Life and Socialism in Mid-Victorian London*, the pubs, coffee houses and clubs in Soho sustained the link of radicalism between the O'Brienites of the Chartist era and the radicals and socialists of the 1870s and onwards.[18] In the 1930s it housed the thriving sheet music and record companies as well as film industry distributors. It was London's best-known red-light district and had significant Chinese and Italian communities. Prior to the Second World War, Soho was often synonymous with "gangland", though after the war it became identified as a new Bohemia, London's answer to the Paris Left Bank or Manhattan's Greenwich Village. Every East End writer made the journey there, even if only for a while.[19]

Ralph Finn was born in Aldgate, in a tenement block in the "Tenterground" and became a journalist in Fleet Street. His first published book, *Down Oxford Street* (1940), was a series of cameos of the people to be found in Oxford Street during lunchtime at the scene of a street accident. Oxford Street, incidentally, marks the northern boundary of Soho. Finn is the only one of the East London writers to consistently portray British fascist character types in his writings. He was a prolific journalist who turned much of his journalism into books, and from 1944 onwards he had a regular column in *The People* newspaper. Most of his writing was based around character sketches and flawed by a sentimentality and a readiness to draw too deeply from the well of pathos. In the 1960s he made his mark again after years of anonymity as a writer with two books of East London reminiscences, *No Tears in Aldgate* (1963), followed by *Spring in Aldgate* (1968). Both are valuable as historical testimony but are flawed by a terrible sentimentalism and moralism.

Roland Camberton (real name Henry Cohen) was born in Hackney, probably around 1918 on the evidence of his auto-biographical novel *Rain on the Pavements*, published in 1951. This is a highly readable account of growing up in a Jewish family in a slightly more prosperous area than Stepney, though only a couple of miles north of it. What is significant is how Camberton's main character David, and his friends, once they begin to write poetry at school and at home, decide they have to spend their time in an appropriate setting. And so, from about the age of fourteen, they walk to Soho every Saturday and Sunday to sit in the coffee bars and soak up the authentic atmosphere "in the wholly fascinating land of Soho". The Soho they are talking about is pre-war Soho, but the setting for Camberton's novel *Scamp* published a year earlier is Soho just after the war.

In many ways *Scamp* is the archetypal novel of the problem of the deracinated writer and has much in common with Goldman's later novels on the same theme. It is the story of a young writer, Ginsberg, who with another would-be writer, Bellinger, lives in a room in an apartment block in Bloomsbury "collecting rejection slips". The parallels with Gissing's *New Grub Street* are quite evident. For Ginsberg,

> ...a story a day, that was his minimum task; two thousand words, preferably with a plot, development, a climax and a twist. After six months of this routine, he was beginning to feel an intense hatred of the short story, in fact, of all writing.

Scamp ends when Ginsberg has been able to inveigle money out of a widow he is privately coaching to start his own literary magazine. The woman gives him the money because it is of some importance and status for her to be able to know a real "writer". The aura of being a "writer" is what keeps Ginsberg and Bellinger alive: their writing doesn't and probably couldn't. The Soho Camberton portrays is peopled by alcoholics, eccentrics, refugees and would-be novelists. There is no sense of a world beyond Soho, or of a country living through a period of economic and social reconstruction and of bitter post-war austerity. The only important problems are inside the writer's head.

Possibly the best-known East London Jewish writer after the war was Wolf Mankowitz. Alone of all these writers he went to university, Cambridge in fact, and there met Raymond Williams with whom he set up the journal *Politics and Letters* in 1947 in Soho, mentioned earlier. The journal only lasted a year but Mankowitz stayed on in Soho and began writing short stories and plays about East London Jewish life, which, for some reason, captured the public mood. *A Kid for Two Farthings*, a moralistic fable about a young boy who befriends a goat which he believes to be a unicorn, set in the East End, and published in 1953 was soon made into a feature film with a full star cast. This happened to another short story, "Make Me An offer", originally published in 1952, which was again made into a full length feature film.

In a way they were ideal stories for a population living through austerity, and for Londoners in particular, many of whom had been uprooted and were living a day-to-day existence. For they were about dreams and luck. They were flights of fancy in which an innocent boy's fantasy affects the lives of all those around him and gilds their lives too, inspiring optimism and a belief in the importance of making the best out of what you have. They were about finding a priceless vase in a junk shop, or in the groundman's cottage rather than in the manor house. The Soho stories were about small ironies of fate and changes in fortune in the lives of the "characters" who lived and worked in Soho. Mankowitz's collection, *Blue Arabian Nights*, which gathered together the stories he wrote while living in Soho are introduced as being about a time when "London was still a suitable Samarkand for a self-made inventor of the long tradition of tellers of a thousand and one curious tales."

Such stories were also to be found in various versions in the London evening newspapers at the time, stories "Out of Court", character sketches of small criminals, or stories from the race-track or the dog-track. This was a period which was fascinated by the spiv and the sad lives of small-time criminals, street traders and eccentric women vagrants; the mood for literature went through a second Dickensian era. Soho was also the home of the nascent pop music industry, which sprang up in response to the wave of excitement surrounding the arrival of American rock-'n'roll music. The "2 Is" cafe in Old Compton Street launched Britain's first home-grown rock'n'roll singer, Tommy Steele, and Wolf Mankowitz wrote a story about it which became a film starring Britain's second rock'n'roll idol, Cliff Richard. The roots of "Swinging London" in the 1960s lay in the journalistic and literary cultivation of Soho in the preceding decades.

The most thoughtful account of this move from working-class Jewish East London to the cosmopolitan, shifting world of Soho is contained in Bernard Kops's *The World Is a Wedding*. One of the most colourful post-war autobiographies, it is a portrait of the pressures and disloca-tions that marked English youth and popular culture after the break-up of the war-time social settlement. Published in 1963, by which time Kops was known as a poet and drama-tist, it is primarily an account of the mental breakdown that follows a long estrangement from his family. They are still living in the East End, while Kops leads an anomic life as a Soho cafe-dweller and drug-user. In the Swiss Cafe in Soho he found "a real sense of security for the first time in years. The characters accepted me just as I was."

Kops was then, like many others, drifting round with "my manuscripts in a carrier bag". One of the rare sources of income in that area was to be got by the buying and selling of second-hand books. Often the first step in capital accumulation in this daily trade was to steal a book from Foyles, which would then be sold for enough money to buy half a dozen second-hand books, which could then be sold separately to buy drink or a cafe meal. At the end of his narrative Kops has become a second-hand book-dealer with a stall just off the Charing Cross Road and reconciled with the members of his family who remain after his mother's death. It is much the best account of Soho in the late 1940s and of its bohemian underworld, though it romanticises what was often a rootless and self-destructive culture. Kops admits, too, that his early interest in writing was awakened by his hours of browsing and reading in the Whitechapel Library.

Finally, there are three other writers who should be mentioned, as they too addressed aspects of Jewish life and culture in East London in the 1930s: Amold Wesker, Alexander Baron and Emanuel Litvinoff. Wesker's trilogy of plays, *Chicken Soup with Barley* (1958), *Roots* (1959), and *I'm Talking About Jerusalem* (1960), follow the fortunes of the same family, from the communist and anti-fascist certainties of the 1930s to the cultural dislocations of the 1950s. These are marked by geographical moves from Stepney to Hackney, and farther still to the middle-class suburbs of north-west London. The trilogy made one of the most stunning contributions to post-war theatre history, accurately and sensitively portraying the ineluctable break-up of what had been a tightly bound community, combining strong familial patterns and connections with a popular loyalty to communist politics. As material circumstances changed, and partly in the light of the Twentieth Soviet Party Congress in 1956 which revealed the terrifying excesses under Stalin, these political ties weakened, and in the move out of East London, political allegiances changed also too.[20]

Alexander Baron grew up in Hackney, outside the classic "East End" where Jewish radicalism flourished, and his development as a writer took a quite different direction. Though active in anti-fascist and Labour youth politics in the 1930s (and with a strong emotional and practical involvement with the cause of the Spanish Republic from 1936 onwards), the major experience which dominated his early novels was that of service life during the Second World War.[21] His understanding of East London politics in the 1930s qualifies the picture which has been passed on in popular mythology in the work of other writers and playwrights. The radicalism and internationalism that marked much Jewish politics in this period was not always shared by the East End working-class in general. The great popular political "moment" of the Battle of Cable Street in 1936, when many trade-union and working-class socialists joined with the Jewish community to prevent the British Union of Fascists marching through East London, has tended to obscure other equally fervent political allegiances in the East End at the time. While many non-Jewish working-class people in East London were loyal to Labour politics, many were equally attracted by the class politics of fascism.[22]

Baron had always rebelled "against the idea of a separate Jewish identity", being like his father and grandfather a freethinker (of the kind T.S. Eliot no doubt feared would destroy English culture).[23] Nevertheless, events conspired to encourage him to produce the *The Lowlife* in 1963, one of the finest novels about Jewish experience, and today the novel for which he is most known.[24] It is a post-war portrait of a middle-aged man — living on his own in a small flat near Stamford Hill, a strongly Jewish district just outside the East End — whose waking life is divided between reading and gambling. It is a detailed study of a type only obliquely referred to in most other novels of Jewish East London, one of the last of the *luftmensches*, those men happier wandering the streets than living or working indoors. Harry Boas, the main character, has sundered most family connections and lives out a self-sufficient life halfway between the old world of the proper East End and the new world of the suburbs. There is also a poignant secondary motif woven into the main story, concerning a youthful affair in Paris, the fathering of an illegitimate child and the disappearance of that child and its mother on a train to Auschwitz.

His novel, *With Hope, Farewell* (1952) tells the story of a young Jew who becomes a pilot during the war, though the opening and closing sections are set in East London, in the late 1920s and the post-war 1940s, and these are very atmospheric in capturing both time and place. The *In-Between Time* (1971) is about Labour League of Youth politics in Hackney during the 1930s and the attempt to get to Spain to fight for the republican cause. Baron's free-thinking Jewish background, and the fact that he grew up outside Jewish East London proper, clearly freed him from the pervasive intensity of that world as described in the writings of Blumenfeld and Goldman, and gave him more fictional distance. He was also indifferent to the attractions of the Bloomsbury literary scene. On the one occasion the publisher Jonathan Cape threw a party for him at Cape's elegant Bedford Square offices, Baron arrived at the door, saw the crowded room, and fled home without entering.[25]

The most recent book evoking that pre-war world is Emanuel Litvinoff's *Journey Through a Small Planet* published in 1972 and written in the form of fully shaped short stories told chronologically.[26] They are very funny, and most of the humour is that of self-deprecation as the narrator sets his own political seriousness and dreams of revolution against the realities of his everyday struggle in life. It is wonderful writing, but its political and aesthetic impulses are those of evocation and nostalgia. For by the time such writers as Ralph Finn and Emanuel Litvinoff decided to set down their accounts of the Jewish East End, they were leading lives in complete contrast to the world they evoked. For them, that quite singular and enormously fertile culture had become, to a large extent, simply the material for a different kind of brilliant and gem-like writing. And the readers who would have recognised their early lives in these books were mostly already in exile themselves. Literature came too late to save politics. The connections had all been broken. The castle had been abandoned.

[1]In an interview I conducted with him at his home on 7 June 1983, Alexander Baron remembered that when he was demobbed at the end of the war, he was asked by the military authorities what he wanted to do in life, and what might he need to help him. "And I said, 'I want a typewriter.' They got me a portable typewriter straight away and I just went home."

[2]William Fishman, *East End Jewish Radicals 1875-1914*, London, 1975.

[3]The Whitechapel Public Library was finally closed in 2003, and a commemorative event was held there at which Bernard Kops paid specific tribute to its undying influence on so many young Jewish intellectuals throughout the twentieth-century.

[4]Jean Liddiard, *Isaac Rosenberg: The Half-Used Life*, London, 1975.

[5]Julius Lipton, *Poems of Strife*, London, 1936.

[6]Stuart Macintyre, *Little Moscows: Communism and Working-Class Militancy in InterWar Britain*, London, 1980.

[7]Blumenfeld's life was richly varied. Born in November 1907, he died on 3 April 2005, at the age of 97. His father's family came from Sicily and his mother was born in Odessa in the Ukraine. He was a great admirer of Israel Zangwill, seeking to emulate him as a serious Jewish writer, though in the 1930s he also wrote Westerns under the name of Huck Messer (the Yiddish term for carving knife). Blumenfeld was a founder of the Stepney Rebel Players, which later became the Unity Theatre after transmigrating to Kings Cross, and he was still a columnist for *The Stage* magazine into his 90s. He was a sharp dresser and lively wit, as was evident at the party held to celebrate the new edition of *Jew Boy* at East Side Bookshop in 1986.

[8]This view is not held by Steven Berkoff, who wrote a glowing introduction to a reprint of *Phineas Kahn* (Lawrence & Wishart, 1988) asserting that, "As a journal of one man which is always fascinating, there are moments when I rank it to stand among the greats, and André-Schwarz-Bart's *The Last of the Just*

springs to mind."

[9]Joe Jacobs, *Out of the Ghetto*, London, 1978, p.38.

[10]Alexander Hartog, *Born to Sing*, London, 1978.

[11]Among the most well known are Jack Dash, unofficial dockers' leader for many years, who also wrote poetry, and whose autobiography *Good Morning Brothers!* was published in 1969, and Stephen Hicks, boxer and poet, whose autobiography, *Sparring For Luck* was published in 1983. A good anthology which represents this tradition is *Bricklight: Poems from the Labour Movement in East London*, (Chris Searle, ed., London, 1980).

[12]Goldman was usually known as Willy Goldman, and published under that name. Some books, however, were published under the name of William Goldman.

[13]Maurice Levinson, *The Trouble With Yesterday*, London, 1946.

[14]I discovered that the definition of literature as "life seen through a temperament" is J.B. Priestley's and comes from his introduction to George Douglas's fine novel, *The House with Green Shutters*, an extraordinary book also sadly neglected.

[15]Raymond Williams, *Politics and Letters*, London, 1979, p.72.

[16]Ruttman's film and its relationship contemporary fiction is discussed in greater detail in the chapter on Hanley, *et al*.

[17]Chaim Lewis, *A Soho Address*, London, 1965.

[18]Stan Shipley, *Club Life and Socialism in Mid-Victorian London*, London, 1972.

[19]Mark Benney's *Low Company* (London 1936) is a classic Soho criminal autobiography. Iain Sinclair's introduction to a new edition of Alexander Baron's *The Lowlife* (2001), describes the post-war drift to Soho particularly well. He also charts how Soho then turned its fashion-conscious attentions to the cobbles, canals and calloused-handed toilers of northern fiction.

[20]A study by Geoffrey Alderman, *The Jewish Community in British Politics*, (Oxford, 1983), revealed that with increased social mobility the Jewish vote had become more conservative.

[21]Baron's work is more fully described in Chapter 3.

[22]In my interview with him, 7 June 1983, Baron observed that "...in the East End of London the real mass politics was fascism and it became a real movement of the people for a period until it all melted away in those great rent strikes." Baron was happy to admit that for a while he had courted a girl who was a Fascist. See also Phil Piratin's *Our Flag Stays Red* (London, 1948) for a full account of the rent strikes in Stepney from 1937 onwards, in

which the Communist Party took an active organising role and was thereby able to check the drift among some tenants towards the British Union of Fascists.

[23]Interview, 7 June 1983.

[24]*The Lowlife* has since been given cult status by the writer Iain Sinclair, amongst others, and Sinclair has provided a thoughtful introduction to a new edition, already mentioned above.

[25]This story is related by Sinclair in his introduction to *The Lowlife* (2001), and by John Williams in his fine obituary of Baron in *The Guardian*, 8 December 1999.

[26]In retrospect, Litvinoff was a much more important writer and influential commentator on Jewish life than I realised at the time. He is known for his trilogy of novels, *A Death out of Season* (1973), *Blood on the Snow* (1975) and *The Face of Terror* (1978), but also for his explosive intervention at a symposium at the Institute of Contemporary Arts in January 1951, when in the presence of T.S. Eliot, Litvinoff read a poem, "To T.S. Eliot", denouncing Eliot's anti-semitism, causing uproar. The full story is told in Dannie Abse's memoir, *A Poet in the Family* (1974), and is further explored in Patrick Wright's appreciation of Litvinoff in *London: City of Disappearances*, (edited Iain Sinclair, 2006). Litvinoff's work is also the subject of an essay by Valentine Cunningham, "Litvinoff's Room: East End Anarchism", in H. Gustav Klaus & Stephen Knight, To *Hell with Culture: Anarchism and Twentieth-Century British Literature* (2005).

Selected Bibliography

Dannie Abse, *A Poet in the Family*, London, 1974.

Walter Allen, *Tradition and Dream*, Harmondsworth, 1965.

Richard D. Altick, *The English Common Reader*, Chicago, 1957.

P.M. Ashraf, *Introduction to Working-Class Literature in Great Britain*, Volumes 1 & 2, Berlin (GDR), 1980.

Alexander Baron, *The Lowlife*, with an introduction by Iain Sinclair, London, 2001

H.E. Bates, *The Vanished World: An Autobiography*, London, 1969.

Ronald Blythe, *Private Words: Letters and Diaries from the Second World War*, Harmondsworth, 1991.

Roland Camberton (Henry Cohen), *Scamp*, London, 1950.

John Carey, *The Intellectuals and the Masses: Pride and Prejudice among the Literary Intelligentsia 1880-1939*, London, 1992.

Claud Cockburn, *Bestseller: The Books That Everyone Read 1900-1939*, London, 1972.

Michael Collins, *The Likes of Us: A Biography of The White Working Class*, London, 2005.

Robert Colls, *Identity of England*, Oxford, 2002.

Andy Croft, *Red Letters: British Fiction in the 1930s*, London, 1990.

Valentine Cunningham, *British Writers of the Thirties*, Oxford, 1988.

William Fishman, *East End Jewish Radicals 1875-1914*, London, 1975.

M.R.D. Foot, *Resistance*, London, 1975.

John Fordham *James Hanley: Modernism and the Working Class,* Cardiff, 2002.

Lynsey Hanley, *Estates: An Intimate History*, London, 2007.

Jenny Hartley, *Millions Like Us: British Women's Fiction of the Second World War*, London, 1997.

Jenny Hartley, *Hearts Undefeated: Women's Writing of the Second World War*, London, 1994.

Jenny Hartley, "Letters Were Everything" in Rebecca Earle, ed., *Epistolary Selves: Letters and Letter-Writers 1600-1945*, Aldershot, 1999.

Robert Hewison, *Under Siege: Literary Life in London 1939-45*,

London, 1979.

Christopher Hilliard, *To Exercise Our Talents: The Democratisation of Writing in Britain*, London, 2006.

Christopher Hilliard, "Modernism and the Common Writer" in *The Historical Journal*, 48, 3, pp.769-787, Cambridge, 2005.

Richard Hoggart, *The Uses of Literacy*, London, 1957.

Humboldt-Universitat, *Working-Class Literature in Britain and Ireland in the 19th and 20th Century, Parts 1 & 2*, Berlin, 1985.

Joe Jacobs, *Out of the Ghetto*, London, 1978.

Anthony Julius, *T.S. Eliot, Anti-Semitism, and Literary Form*, Cambridge, 1995.

H Gustav Klaus & Stephen Knight, *To Hell with Culture: Anarchism and Twentieth-century British Literature*, Cardiff, 2005.

Bernard Kops, *The World is a Wedding*, London, 1963.

Nella Last, *Nella Last's Diary 1939-45*, edited by Richard Broad & Suzie Fleming, Bristol, 1981.

John Lucas, *The Radical Twenties: Aspects of Writing, Politics and Culture*, Nottingham, 1997.

Alan Munton, *English Fiction of the Second World War*, London, 1989.

Ross McKibbin, *The Ideologies of Class: Social Relations in Britain 1880-1950*, Clarendon Press, Oxford, 1990.

Rebecca O'Rourke, "Were there no women?", *Literature and History*, Vol 14, No 1, p.48-63. Spring 2005.

Adam Piette, *Imagination at War: British Fiction and Poetry 1939-1945*, London, 1995.

Mark Rawlinson, *British Writing of the Second World War*, Oxford, 2000.

Valerie A. Reeves and Valerie Showan, *Dan Billany: Hull's Lost Hero*, Hull, 1999.

Jonathan Rose, *The Intellectual Life of the British Working Classes*, London, 2001.

Sukhdev Sandhu, *London Calling: How Black and Asian Writers Imagined a City*, London, 2003.

Dorothy Sheridan, *Wartime Women: An Anthology of Women's Wartime Writing for Mass Observation*, London, 1990.

Iain Sinclair, *London: City of Disappearances*, London, 2006.

Ken Worpole, *Reading By Numbers: Contemporary Publishing and Popular Fiction*, London, 1984.